YOUR GUIDE T[illegible]

F[illegible]
VEGETABLES
AND NUTS

Isobel Skypala

Series Editor: Susan Lewis

WISEBUY PUBLICATIONS

First published 1987

Further copies of FRUIT, VEGETABLES AND NUTS can be obtained from Wisebuy Publications, PO Box 379, London NW3 1NJ, price £1.50 plus 50p p+p (UK) or £4 airmail including p+p.

ISBN 0-9509751-4-1

Typesetting by MC Typeset Ltd., Chatham, Kent
Reproduced, printed and bound in Great Britain by
Hazell Watson & Viney Limited,
Member of the BPCC Group,
Aylesbury, Bucks

Contents

About the author

Isobel Skypala is Chief Dietician at the Brompton Hospital, one of three London hospitals which form the National Heart and Chest Hospitals Group.

Over the last seven years at the Brompton, she has been involved in all dietary aspects of heart disease and the management of food allergies. She has also carried out major research work with young people suffering from cystic fibrosis.

Isobel Skypala has a degree in nutrition and dietetics from Leeds Polytechnic where she qualified in 1979.

Isobel would like to thank her dietetic colleagues and her sister, Pauline, for all their advice and help.

1

Food facts

Eating a healthy diet has never been easier. The variety of foods available today is huge compared with even ten years ago. But this increase in choice has brought great confusion about which foods to choose and how much to eat. The aim of these guides is to give you an easy way to find out what you are getting from your daily food intake and to help you to make a healthier food choice.

Fortunately many doctors, dieticians and others involved in health education are now in agreement about what constitutes a healthy diet. Reports have been produced giving facts and figures and some of the myths about food are beginning to disappear. However it is hard for most people to translate some of these health messages into practical hints for every day eating.

To help you help yourself and your family, Chapters 1 to 3 describe what you need to know about the different nutrients in food such as protein, fat, sugar, fibre, minerals and vitamins. Chapter 4 tells you how much of each nutrient the experts in the UK and the USA suggest you should eat each day. And Chapter 5 contains over 100 food tables which show the nutritional contents of average servings of fruit, vegetables and nuts. Other foods will be covered shortly in two companion guides.

Calories

A calorie is a measure of energy and the calorie value of a food indicates how much energy that food provides after you have eaten it. Most foods contain calories in the form of protein, fat, carbohydrate, and sometimes alcohol, but not in equal proportions. Compared to protein and carbohydrate, fat provides twice the number of calories. Vitamins and minerals do not have a calorie value.

For a healthy diet, it is important that your calorie intake comes from a variety of foods. Although protein can be used to provide calories, its main function is the promotion of tissue growth and repair. So it is important not only to eat enough calories, but also make sure a sufficient number of those calories comes from carbohydrate and fat.

Everyone needs a different number of calories, depending on their age, sex, and occupation. Even if you are just lying down and doing nothing, your body still uses up about half of your daily calorie intake. Women usually use less calories than men while resting and you also need less the older you get.

The rest of your calorie requirement depends on the amount of energy you use up during the day. Everyone has very different energy needs and they may not match the recommended intakes. If you are fit and well and not overweight there is no need to worry if you are eating a lot more than the recommended intake. However, remember that your requirements will change as you grow older.

Currently 35% to 39% of the population are overweight and so much more likely to develop heart disease and diabetes. If you are overweight, the sensible way to try and lose it is to eat small regular meals and avoid a lot of fried and sugary foods, and alcohol. It is also important to take some exercise such as swimming, cycling or brisk walking. Taking moderate exercise three to four times a week is better than very vigorous exercise once a week. Even just walking to the next bus stop, or climbing the stairs instead of taking the lift or escalator helps to use up calories.

Protein

The amount of food eaten in the UK has decreased this century but the proportion of protein has remained the same. A lot of protein comes from animal sources such as meat, fish, eggs, cheese, and milk. However quite a lot also comes from vegetables sources such as peas, beans, lentils, cereals and nuts.

People usually eat more protein than the recommended intake but this is not thought to be harmful. Recent guidelines suggest a healthy diet should contain more protein from fish, vegetables and cereals, and less from red meat and milk products. So although protein intakes would stay the same, the diet would contain less fat and more starchy carbohydrate.

Vegans, who eat no animal protein at all, need to make sure that they are having a good mixture of vegetable and cereal protein. Well balanced vegetarian and vegan diets can be very nourishing and healthy, since they are usually quite low in fat and high in fibre.

Protein is needed for growth and development. A new baby needs five times more protein per kilogram of body weight than an adult. This requirement becomes less as the child develops and the growth rate slows down. A deficiency of protein is rare in children in this country but affects many children in third world countries, who have low calorie intakes and use protein for energy and not for growth and development.

However, one group of people in the UK who might develop protein deficiency are the elderly, especially those who live alone. Although they have the lowest requirement, they often eat very little protein because of low incomes, poor cooking facilities and infirmity.

These days more people are involved in fitness training where emphasis is often placed on diet particularly protein. People in training often eat up to 5,000 calories a day, a lot of which comes from large amounts of protein. Although your calorie requirement goes up during training, your need for protein does not and eating large amounts of protein has no effect on athletic performance.

Fat

There are three main categories of fat: saturated, polyunsaturated and mono-unsaturated.

Saturated fats are usually animal fats and tend to be solid at room temperature. This group includes milk fats like butter, cheese, cream and milk; meat fat like lard and suet; eggs; and many margarines.

Polyunsaturated fats usually come from vegetables and are often liquid at room temperature. They include sunflower, safflower, soya and corn oils; polyunsaturated margarines; and fish oils.

The most common mono-unsaturated fats are olive oil, peanut oil and rapeseed oil.

Most foods containing fat include a mixture of these three types of fat. All three types contain the same number of calories.

Nearly half people's calorie intake (42%) comes from fat. Although total calorie intake has in many cases fallen over the last 100 years, the percentage of calories coming from fat has increased. This means we are eating less starchy carbohydrate and therefore less fibre. This change in eating habits is thought to be one of the causes of diseases such as heart disease and bowel cancer.

During the 1939–1945 world war when food was rationed, only 33% of calorie intake came from fat. This is now thought to be the amount a healthy diet should provide and to achieve this most people need to cut down substantially on their fat intake.

Studies have shown that a diet high in fat, especially saturated fat, raises the level of cholesterol in the blood. Cholesterol is a product of fat digestion. A high blood cholesterol level is one of the risk factors for heart disease. Polyunsaturated fat can lower blood cholesterol levels but its effect is only half as strong as the cholesterol-raising ability of saturated fat.

Currently half of people's fat intake comes from saturated fat and only one eighth from polyunsaturated fat. So as well as reducing your total fat intake, you should also consider the type of fat you eat.

If you wish to control your fat intake, think about both visible and hidden fats. Visible fats include butter, cream, margarine and cooking oils. Fat is also hidden in cakes, biscuits, pastry and many other foods, as you will see when you check through the food descriptions. Changing from ordinary milk to semi-skimmed or skimmed milk, and using thinly-spread polyunsaturated margarine or a low-fat spread will reduce your fat intake. Eating less cheese and red meat, and more chicken, fish and vegetable dishes, as well as low fat cheese, will also help.

Carbohydrates

Sugar, starch and fibre are the three main types of carbohydrates. Throughout the world they provide most of the energy in the diet. In poor countries 90% of the calories may come from carbohydrates whilst in affluent countries it might only be 40%.

Sugar

The most simple of all the carbohydrates are the sugars which include glucose, fructose (fruit sugar), sucrose (sugar and beet sugar) and lactose (milk sugar). Sugar intake in the UK reached a maximum in 1974 when the average sugar intake was 2lbs a week. Although this has gone down over the last decade, it is still causing concern and some reports suggest people should halve their current intake. Sugar has been linked to dental decay.

The reason why so much sugar is eaten is partly that it is a good preservative and used in many different foods. A high sugar content helps to extend the shelf-life of food by stopping the growth of moulds. People develop a sweet tooth if they become accustomed to sweet foods early on in life.

Pure sugar only gives you calories although honey and some of the very dark brown sugars contain very small amounts of minerals. Cutting down on sugar will help you lose weight without missing out on any essential nutrients. Many people believe sugars such as honey to have restorative properties. There is no evidence that honey or brown sugar are good for you or any better than white sugar. A well balanced diet provides all the calories most people, including children, need.

The best way to start eating less sugar is by gradually reducing the amount you add so that your taste buds will get used to a less sweet taste. Using a sugar substitute will not help you lose your sweet tooth. Cut down on sweets and chocolates especially in between meals. Avoid soft drinks and squashes sweetened with sugar. Even unsweetened natural fruit juice contains sugar from the fruit so dilute it if you normally drink a lot. Check food labels to see how high sugar comes on the list of ingredients. If it is near the top, or listed in several different ways (sucrose, glucose, honey), you can be sure that the product contains a lot of sugar.

Starch

The second main type of carbohydrate is starch which is broken down into glucose in the body and found in cereals such as wheat and rice and some vegetables. In the past many 'slimming' diets have recommended that starchy foods should be eaten in small amounts or even cut out completely. Now reducing diets encourage people to eat normal or only slightly smaller amounts of starchy foods and to avoid fatty and sugary foods.

Bread, potatoes and other starchy foods can provide significant amounts of protein, iron, calcium and vitamin C. Today's guidelines to cut down on fat will mean eating more of these starchy foods.

Fibre

Fibre or roughage is found in the indigestible fibrous parts of fruit and vegetables such as the stalk, skin, leaves, and core, and the husk of cereal grains. Over the last century our fibre intake has fallen by two thirds and most of us only eat 20 g. a day compared to people living in rural Africa who eat between 50 g. to 120 g. of fibre a day.

This falling intake has been linked with an increase in such problems as constipation, bowel cancer and heart disease. So most recent medical reports say fibre intakes should be increased to 30 g. a day. You should not do this by just taking large amounts of wheat bran and not changing your diet, as this can create more problems than it solves.

You can easily increase your fibre intake by changing to wholemeal bread and by eating plenty of fresh fruit and vegetables, raw and well washed with the skins on where possible. Try porridge or a wholegrain breakfast cereal but remember to check the label for sugar content. Beans and lentils contain a lot of fibre. Dried beans should be soaked and boiled for ten minutes before slow cooking. If you eat a lot of pasta or rice you should try the wholegrain varieties as they are much tastier.

Remember to drink plenty of fluids when you increase your intake of fibre since it is very absorbent.

2

Minerals

Calcium

Your body contains a great deal of calcium in bones and teeth, so a good intake is important, especially for children, expectant and nursing mothers, and the elderly. You need more calcium when young because in a young child the skeleton is replaced completely within one to two years. In adults, this replacement continues, but much more slowly, until the age of 40 when the bones gradually begin to break down. Before birth, and during breast feeding, the calcium needs of the baby are met by a supply from the mother. So if the mother is not eating enough calcium she will become deficient.

Most calcium in the diet comes from milk, skimmed milk having the same amount as full cream milk. Other sources are cheese, water in hard water areas, and tinned fish containing bones, such as pilchards and sardines. Calcium is often added to flour, so bread can be an important source for some people. Soya milk may also be fortified with calcium.

In the UK calcium intakes are often much higher than the recommended intake because of all the milk and cheese eaten. High calcium intakes are not harmful, but there is probably nothing to be gained from eating more than 1,000 mg. a day.

Iron

Iron is found in both animal and vegetable food groups. A lack of iron in the diet causes a blood disorder called iron-deficiency anaemia, which is still relatively common in the UK. People most likely to be affected are women of child bearing age, particularly those who do not eat meat or eggs.

Foods rich in iron in a form that is easily used by the body include liver, red meat, and blood products such as black pudding and haggis. Reasonable amounts of iron are also found in eggs, oats, wholemeal bread, chocolate, treacle, pulses, and some green vegetables. Because the body only absorbs 10% of its iron intake, you should eat the recommended daily amounts given in Chapter 4 to ensure you get enough.

The iron found in eggs and vegetables is not as easily used as that found in meat and offal, but vitamin C helps the body to absorb both sources of iron. Recent reports suggest that the best way to increase iron intake and prevent deficiency, is by eating more fruit and vegetables to aid iron absorption, rather than by eating more meat which is high in fat.

Zinc

Much is still to be learned about this mineral but we know it is part of several substances known as enzymes, without which necessary reactions cannot take place in the body. Zinc is found in many foods but meat and unmilled cereals are particularly good sources.

It is quite rare for anyone in Britain to develop zinc deficiency, although diets which are very high in cereal fibre may cause deficiency due to the binding of zinc by a substance called phytate which is present in wheat bran and which prevents the absorption of zinc in the body. The average British diet provides about 10 mg. of zinc a day. There is no UK recommended daily intake but the USA has a recommended daily intake of 15 mg. a day, which is 50% higher than the average UK intake.

There are however a few people who might benefit from zinc supplements. Small-for-date babies may have mothers who have low blood zinc levels, so supplementation during pregnancy may be important especially for vegetarians. Extra zinc might also help leg ulcers to heal more quickly in people who have low blood levels. People who have a poor food intake such as the elderly, or those who have cancer, are often unable to taste and smell food normally which might be due to a lack of dietary zinc. It could also be important to supplement the diets of people who cannot absorb food properly.

Copper

If you eat a variety of foods grown in different areas, you are unlikely to become deficient in copper. The daily diet contains about 2.5 mg. of copper, most of which comes from green vegetables, fish and liver. Copper plays a part in the formation of blood.

Copper deficiency usually only occurs in a genetically inherited condition where the sufferer cannot absorb copper. Premature babies may develop copper deficiency unless they are fed on a proper modified baby milk, since cows milk is a very poor source of copper.

Sodium and salt

Sodium is probably one of the most widespread nutrients in food, but the amount naturally present is small. Foods which contain a lot of sodium have usually had it added in the form of sodium bicarbonate or salt (sodium chloride). One gram of salt contains 388 mg. of sodium. Sodium is an essential part of all body cells, but the average daily intake of salt is 12 times higher than the one gram of salt needed each day to meet sodium requirements. Luckily, the body has the ability to lose most of this excess sodium in the urine.

Because most people eat more sodium than they need, the effect of sodium on blood pressure has been closely studied. It is still not clear whether cutting salt intakes will lower blood pressure in everyone, but there is an effect in people who already have high blood pressure. In Britain, one person in five is likely to develop high blood pressure.

If you want to eat less salt, look for foods which contain only small amounts naturally. All fresh foods are suitable. It will help to avoid meat products such as sausages, bacon, ham and pâté, and cured fish such as kippers and smoked haddock. Look for vegetables which are not tinned in brine, and try low salt baked beans. Tinned soups and bottled sauces are also high in salt.

A third of your salt intake is added during cooking and at the table. If you want to add less salt to food, it is easier to stop adding it at the table and still add a small amount during cooking. It will take time to get used to food without added salt so persevere and leave the salt cellar in the cupboard.

Potassium

Potassium is an essential part of muscle tissue in the body. It is very rare for most people to either need extra potassium or to reduce the amount they eat, except when they have specific medical conditions, or are on particular drugs which rid the body of too much potassium.

Potassium is lost from the body in much the same way as sodium and the amount you lose is small and corresponds to the amount you eat. Potassium is closely associated with protein so if body muscle is being broken down and lost more potassium will be needed.

Potassium is found in a wide variety of foods, fruit, vegetables and meat being the best sources.

Magnesium

Together with calcium, magnesium is another important part of bone and half the amount contained in the body is found in the skeleton. It also plays a part in many reactions which take place in the body and all human tissue contains small amounts of magnesium.

Most foods contain some magnesium, particularly green vegetables, since magnesium is an essential part of the green colour chlorophyll. Cereals and vegetables between them contribute more than two thirds of the daily magnesium intake. Meat and offal are also good sources.

Phosphorus

Phosphorus is present in all natural foods as it is a major part of all plant and animal cells. Generally foods which are high in calcium and protein are also rich in phosphorus. It is also used as a food additive and 10% of the phosphorus eaten has been added artificially. Deficiency is unknown in man because of its wide distribution.

Most of the phosphorus in the body is found in the bones, and the kidneys control the level in the blood. In the past, the only concern with phosphorus has been with very young babies being fed on cows milk, which contains more phosphorus than breast milk. However there is now a wide range of modified baby milks for those babies not being breast fed.

3

Vitamins

Vitamin A

Vitamin A is found in both animal and vegetable foods. The animal source is a substance called retinol, which is present in full cream milk, butter, cheese, egg yolk, liver and some of the fatty fish. The richest natural sources of retinol are fish liver oils such as cod liver oil.

The vegetable source is called beta carotene which is converted to retinol inside the body. The amount of retinol yielded from beta carotene is only one sixth of its original weight. Green vegetables such as cabbage and lettuce contain a lot of carotene but only in the dark outer leaves. Yellow and red fruits and vegetables, especially carrots, also contain good amounts of carotene. Vegetable oils contain no beta carotene except for red palm oil. In the UK vitamin A is added to margarine.

Vitamin A is essential for vision in dim light but it is very unusual for anyone in the Western World to suffer from a deficiency. One of the reasons why deficiency is so rare is that this vitamin can be stored in the liver. Most people store 90 mg. to 150 mg. which is enough to meet normal requirements for months or even years, without eating any more. Occasionally these stores can get low, particularly in old age when people may not eat as well. Because vitamin A is stored, taking extra amounts can cause side effects and very large amounts are dangerous.

Vitamin C

Vitamin C is mainly found in fruit and vegetables. Good sources include citrus fruits, blackcurrants, strawberries and kiwi fruit. For many people, potatoes provide most of their vitamin C intake because although they only contain moderate amounts of the vitamin, they are usually eaten in larger quantities than most other vegetables and fruit.

Vitamin C prevents scurvy, increases the absorption of iron, and helps wounds to heal. It might also have a role to play in the prevention of gastric cancer and strokes, and in the lowering of blood cholesterol levels. The recommended intake in the UK is 30 mg. a day. This was originally calculated by building in a threefold safety margin to the 10 mg. a day which was found to prevent scurvy. However, the recommended intake in other countries is much higher, particularly the USA where it is 60 mg.

Most people eat more than 30 mg. a day although 10% of households in the UK have been estimated to consume less. Recently, some people have been taking many times the UK recommended intake of vitamin C in order to prevent a variety of illnesses including the common cold. Since at this high dosage most of the vitamin does not appear to be absorbed, it is not clear whether this type of therapy is effective or whether it might even be harmful in the long term.

Vitamin D

The amount of vitamin D that occurs naturally in food is small and restricted to very few foods such as oily fish, eggs, liver and kidneys. Some foods such as margarine are fortified with the manufactured form of the vitamin.

However, most of the vitamin D in the body does not come from food but is the product of a reaction which takes place when skin is exposed to sunlight. It is produced by the action of ultra-violet light on a substance found in the oily secretions of human skin.

Vitamin D, like vitamin A, is stored in the liver and kidneys, which is useful since less is produced in the winter because there is less sunlight. Vitamin D is necessary for the formation of normal bones and is involved in controlling the amount of calcium in the blood. It takes calcium from the bones if there is not enough in the blood and acts in response to the body's changing need for calcium.

Too little vitamin D will cause joint problems and bone deformities, particularly in the young and old, even if the diet contains enough calcium, since it cannot be used without the action of vitamin D. Expectant mothers should have good intakes of the vitamin even before they conceive as babies lay down a reserve of vitamin D from the mother before they are born. Elderly housebound people often have low levels of vitamin D because of a poor food intake and lack of sunshine. Some groups of Asians, particularly women, may also need more possibly because they have less exposure to sunlight.

Vitamin D can have toxic effects at high doses but this only applies to oral vitamin D as the body regulates against overproduction of vitamin D from sunshine. An intake of only 50 µg. a day over a period of time is known to be toxic. The recommended intake for most people is 10 µg. a day.

Vitamin E

Good sources of vitamin E are vegetable oils, nuts, oily fish like tuna, egg, wholewheat cereals, avocado pear and spinach.

Vitamin E has a protective effect on polyunsaturated fats both in food and in the body. It is found in all your cell membranes and may have a role in preventing a large number of degenerative disorders. Your requirement depends on the amount of polyunsaturated fat you eat. Western diets provide 5 mg. to 10 mg. a day and some people appear to maintain good health on a quarter of this amount. For this reason there is no recommended daily intake in the UK for this vitamin although the USA has one of 8 mg. to 10 mg. a day for most adults.

People who might need extra vitamin E are those with liver problems or who cannot digest fats. It has also been recommended in the treatment of many conditions including sterility and skin disorders, as well as to delay aging and improve sexual function. There is still no real evidence that it can improve any of these.

B Vitamin Complex

Vitamin B1

Also known as thiamin, good amounts of vitamin B1 are found in meat, particularly pork, wholewheat products, potatoes and some nuts. Yeast extract, fish, beans and other pulses are also good sources. If sugar cane and cereals are refined, the vitamin is lost and so many manufactured foods such as breakfast cereals have the vitamin added. Because vitamin B1 is soluble in water much can be lost during cooking especially if sodium bicarbonate is added to the water. So only use a small amount of water or better still steam vegetables or cook them in a microwave oven.

Vitamin B1 is concerned with the breakdown of carbohydrate in the body. A small amount is stored but most is lost in the urine. Since it cannot be accumulated, it is almost impossible to take too much. Although the UK recommended figure is one of the lowest in Europe, it is believed to be adequate.

Vitamin B2

Liver, kidney, yeast extracts, milk and eggs, are all good sources of vitamin B2 also known as riboflavin. It is also found in beer. Some foods are fortified with it. Vitamin B2 is soluble in water and although ordinary cooking methods will not completely destroy it by heat, it is often thrown away with the water the food is cooked in. It is also destroyed by ultra-violet light and most vitamin B2 contained in milk will be lost if it is left on the doorstep all day.

In the UK, vitamin B2 deficiency is not common except amongst people who have a very poor food intake or follow a very restricted diet.

Niacin

Niacin, also known as nicotinic acid and vitamin B3, is found in many foods but only in small amounts. Meat, liver, offal, fish, wholemeal cereals and beans are the best sources. Some processed foods have it added. Unlike other B vitamins, the body can make niacin from certain high protein foods such as milk and eggs. Heat does not destroy this vitamin but large amounts can be lost in the cooking water since it is water soluble.

Many cereals contain large amounts of niacin but it is useless because it is present in a bound form and only treatment with an alkaline substance can release it. Niacin can easily be produced synthetically and also occurs naturally in the body in the form of nicotinamide. It is related chemically to nicotine but behaves very differently and is not harmful even in large amounts. Pellagra, the condition caused by a lack of niacin, is very rare in this country.

Vitamin B6

The average British diet provides about 2 mg. of vitamin B6 a day. This vitamin is also known as pyridoxine. Meat, liver, wholewheat cereals and some vegetables contain the most. Many countries including the UK do not give a recommended daily intake figure for this vitamin since it is so widely distributed in food. However the USA do have a recommended intake of 2 mg. to 2.2 mg. a day for adults.

It is very rare for anyone to develop a deficiency of vitamin B6 except in association with another disorder such as severe malnutrition. But some women taking oral contraceptives may get relief from headaches and sickness by taking extra vitamin B6. Also some women find that premenstrual tension is helped by taking quite large amounts of this vitamin, sometimes up to 200 mg. a day. This beneficial effect has yet to be proved by scientific research.

Vitamin B12

Vitamin B12 is unique because it is not found in any plants. Sources include liver, kidney, sardines, oysters, heart, rabbit, meat, eggs, cheese, and milk. Estimated intakes of vitamin B12 range from 3 μg. to 32 μg. a day in the UK. So people who eat a mixed diet will take in more than the normal requirement of 2 μg. to 4 μg. a day, as will vegetarians who eat milk and dairy products. Vegans who eat no animal foods often need to take fortified yeast extracts or get their vitamin B12 from the moulds which contaminate food. Vitamin B12 is the only B vitamin that can be stored in large amounts in the liver, most adults having a five year supply.

Folic acid

There are very few rich natural sources of this vitamin, green vegetables and liver being the two main ones. Folic acid is lost from food if it is stored for a long time, exposed to light or cooked. So store vegetables in a dim light and eat as soon as possible.

A normal diet contains about 100 μg. to 300 μg. a day and although only a quarter of this is completely absorbed, it is thought to cover most people's requirements in the UK. No daily amounts are officially recommended in the UK but in the USA 400 μg. a day is recommended and this rises to 800 μg. a day during pregnancy.

A lack of folic acid can cause a type of anaemia. This is unlikely to happen in most people but some need extra folic acid such as pregnant women, the elderly and certain groups of Asians. If women have folic acid deficiency before they conceive, it is possible they are more likely to have babies with malformations of the central nervous system, such as spina bifida. Therefore, since folic acid requirements increase during pregnancy, it is important that the diet is already rich in folic acid before conception. Blood levels of folic acid are lower in old people than in younger ages. This means some elderly people may become deficient if they do not eat enough food containing this vitamin.

Pantothenic acid

This vitamin is present in all living things and is so widely distributed in natural foods that a deficiency is unlikely. The only people who might develop one are those who eat mostly processed foods. Most pantothenic acid is found in liver, kidney, yeast, egg yolk, and fresh vegetables. Cooking will destroy pantothenic acid but only if the temperature goes above boiling point. Frozen foods especially meat will lose a lot during thawing. There is no good reason for taking extra. Although a lack of the vitamin causes the greying of hair in rats, supplements will not prevent the development of grey hair in man.

Biotin

Biotin can be found in a variety of foods, liver, kidney and yeast extract being the best sources. The human body uses only a few micrograms of biotin daily and can usually get all it needs from the many micro-organisms that are present in food or living in the intestines.

A deficiency of biotin cannot occur naturally in man and all recorded instances of a deficiency have been associated with the consumption of raw eggs, either in excess, or to the exclusion of all other foods. The reason for this is that raw egg contains a protein which combines with biotin and makes it unusable. Cooking the egg changes the protein structure and the vitamin is released.

4

What the experts suggest

There are two main sets of dietary guidelines and these are summarised in the tables of this chapter. The first are the official recommended daily amounts (RDAs) of certain nutrients for different age groups and sex. Every country has its own figures and the UK recommendations by the Department of Health and Social Security (DHSS), last revised in 1979, are given together with those recommended in the USA in 1980 by the Food and Nutrition Board, National Academy of Sciences – National Research Council.

The second set of dietary guidelines come from various reports produced by groups of experts. These reports do not cover all nutrients but give recommendations on specific aspects and often describe how dietary changes can be achieved.

The most important report of the 1980s was the NACNE report and its recommendations are also summarised on the following pages. This report was a discussion paper on proposals for nutritional guidelines for health education in Britain produced by the Health Education Council in 1983. Another significant report was one on diet and cardiovascular disease, known as the COMA report, which was produced by the DHSS in 1984. The most recent report on diet, nutrition and health was produced by the British Medical Association in 1986.

Only use the following recommendations as a guide. Different people may need different amounts. A dash (–) means no recommendations have been made.

Children aged one to six years

UK Official recommended daily amounts unless otherwise stated.

Food Facts

Energy 1,100 to 1,740 kcal.
Protein 27 to 43 g.
Total fat –
Saturated fat –
Polyunsaturated fat –
Carbohydrate –
Sugars –
Fibre –

Minerals

Calcium 600 mg.
Iron 8 mg.
Zinc –
Copper –
Sodium –
Potassium –
Magnesium –
Phosphorus –

Vitamins

Vitamin A 300 μg.
Vitamin C 20 mg.
Vitamin D 10 μg.
Vitamin E –
Vitamin B1 0.5 mg.
Vitamin B2 0.75 mg.
Niacin 8.5 mg.
Vitamin B6 –
Vitamin B12 –
Folic acid –
Pantothenic acid –
Biotin –

Children's requirements are very varied so only use these figures as a guide.

USA Official recommended daily amounts unless otherwise stated.

Food Facts

Energy 1,300 to 1,700 kcal.
Protein 23 to 30 g.
Total fat –
Saturated fat –
Polyunsaturated fat –
Carbohydrate –
Sugars –
Fibre –

Minerals

Calcium 800 mg.
Iron 12.5 mg.
Zinc 10 mg.
Copper –
Sodium –
Potassium –
Magnesium 175 mg.
Phosphorus 800 mg.

Vitamins

Vitamin A 450 μg.
Vitamin C 45 mg.
Vitamin D 10 μg.
Vitamin E 5.5 mg.
Vitamin B1 0.8 mg.
Vitamin B2 0.9 mg.
Niacin 10 mg.
Vitamin B6 1.1 μg.
Vitamin B12 2.25 μg.
Folic acid 150 μg.
Pantothenic acid –
Biotin –

Young children need varied healthy meals, not a very low fat, high fibre diet. Give them full cream milk and butter, not low fat substitutes.

Children aged seven to 12 years

UK Official recommended daily amounts unless otherwise stated.

Food Facts

Energy 1,900 to 2,280 kcal.
Protein 47 to 57 g.
Total fat –
Saturated fat –
Polyunsaturated fat –
Carbohydrate –
Sugars –
Fibre –

Minerals

Calcium 650 mg.
Iron 11 mg.
Zinc –
Copper –
Sodium –
Potassium –
Magnesium –
Phosphorus –

Vitamins

Vitamin A 487 μg.
Vitamin C 22.5 mg.
Vitamin D 10 μg.
Vitamin E –
Vitamin B1 0.85 mg.
Vitamin B2 1.1 mg.
Niacin 12.5 mg.
Vitamin B6 –
Vitamin B12 –
Folic acid –
Pantothenic acid –
Biotin –

Children's requirements are very varied so only use these figures as a guide.

USA Official recommended daily amounts unless otherwise stated.

Food Facts

Energy 2,400 to 2,700 kcal.
Protein 34 to 45 g.
Total fat –
Saturated fat –
Polyunsaturated fat –
Carbohydrate –
Sugars –
Fibre –

Minerals

Calcium 1,000 mg.
Iron 10 to 18 mg.
Zinc 12.5 mg.
Copper –
Sodium –
Potassium –
Magnesium 300 mg.
Phosphorus 1,000 mg.

Vitamins

Vitamin A 850 μg.
Vitamin C 47.5 mg.
Vitamin D 10 μg.
Vitamin E 7.5 mg.
Vitamin B1 1.3 mg.
Vitamin B2 1.5 mg.
Niacin 17 mg.
Vitamin B6 1.7 mg.
Vitamin B12 3 μg.
Folic acid 350 μg.
Pantothenic acid –
Biotin –

Adults develop a taste for sweet and salty foods in childhood so don't add extra salt or sugar to children's food.

Teenagers aged 13 to 18 years

UK Official recommended daily amounts unless otherwise stated.

Food Facts

Energy 2,150 to 2,880 kcal.
Protein 53 to 72 g.
Total fat –
Saturated fat –
Polyunsaturated fat –
Carbohydrate –
Sugars –
Fibre –

Minerals

Calcium 650 mg.
Iron 12 mg.
Zinc –
Copper –
Sodium –
Potassium –
Magnesium –
Phosphorus –

Vitamins

Vitamin A 737 μg.
Vitamin C 27 mg.
Vitamin D 10 μg.
Vitamin E –
Vitamin B1 1.02 mg.
Vitamin B2 1.55 mg.
Niacin 17.5 mg.
Vitamin B6 –
Vitamin B12 –
Folic acid –
Pantothenic acid –
Biotin –

Young people's requirements are very varied so only use these figures as a guide.

USA Official recommended daily amounts unless otherwise stated.

Food Facts

Energy 2,750 kcal.
Protein 45 to 56 g.
Total fat –
Saturated fat –
Polyunsaturated fat –
Carbohydrate –
Sugars –
Fibre –

Minerals

Calcium 1,200 mg.
Iron 18 mg.
Zinc 15 mg.
Copper –
Sodium –
Potassium –
Magnesium 337 mg.
Phosphorus 1,200 mg.

Vitamins

Vitamin A 900 μg.
Vitamin C 55 mg.
Vitamin D 10 μg.
Vitamin E 8.5 mg.
Vitamin B1 1.25 mg.
Vitamin B2 1.3 to 1.7 mg.
Niacin 16.2 mg.
Vitamin B6 1.9 mg.
Vitamin B12 3 μg.
Folic acid 400 μg.
Pantothenic acid –
Biotin –

If teenagers will not eat proper meals, wholemeal toasted sandwiches or jacket potatoes with various fillings are good substitutes.

Women aged 19 to 54 years

UK Official recommended daily amounts unless otherwise stated.

Food Facts
Energy 2,150 kcal.
Protein 54 g.
Total fat 69 g.[1]
Saturated fat 23 g.[1]
Polyunsaturated fat 11.5 g.[1]
Carbohydrate 286 g.[1]
Sugars 50 g.[1]
Fibre 30 g.[1]

Minerals
Calcium 500 mg.
Iron 12 mg.
Zinc –
Copper –
Sodium 3,496 mg. (9 g. salt)[1]
Potassium –
Magnesium –
Phosphorus –

Vitamins
Vitamin A 750 μg.
Vitamin C 30 mg.
Vitamin D 10 μg.
Vitamin E –
Vitamin B1 0.9 mg.
Vitamin B2 1.3 mg.
Niacin 15 mg.
Vitamin B6 –
Vitamin B12 –
Folic acid –
Pantothenic acid –
Biotin –

[1]Recommended in the NACNE report produced by the Health Education Council in 1983.

USA Official recommended daily amounts unless otherwise stated.

Food Facts
Energy 2,050 kcal.
Protein 44 g.
Total fat 66 g.[2]
Saturated fat 22 g.[2]
Polyunsaturated fat 22 g.[2]
Carbohydrate 262 g.[2]
Sugars 54 g.[2]
Fibre –

Minerals
Calcium 800 mg.
Iron 18 mg.
Zinc 15 mg.
Copper –
Sodium 1,942 mg. (5 g. salt)[2]
Potassium –
Magnesium 300 mg.
Phosphorus 800 mg.

Vitamins
Vitamin A 800 μg.
Vitamin C 60 mg.
Vitamin D 6.25 μg.
Vitamin E 8 mg.
Vitamin B1 1.05 mg.
Vitamin B2 1.25 mg.
Niacin 13.5 mg.
Vitamin B6 2 mg.
Vitamin B12 3 μg.
Folic acid 400 μg.
Pantothenic acid –
Biotin –

[2]Recommended in a report called Dietary Goals for the United States, produced by the U.S. Senate Committee on nutrition in 1977.

Pregnant women

UK Official recommended daily amounts unless otherwise stated.

Food Facts
Energy 2,400 kcal.
Protein 60 g.
Total fat 77 g.[1]
Saturated fat 25 g.[1]
Polyunsaturated fat 12 g.[1]
Carbohydrate 320 g.[1]
Sugars 50 g.[1]
Fibre 30 g.[1]

Minerals
Calcium 1,200 mg.
Iron 13 mg.
Zinc –
Copper –
Sodium 3,496 mg. (9 g. salt)[1]
Potassium –
Magnesium –
Phosphorus –

Vitamins
Vitamin A 750 μg.
Vitamin C 60 mg.
Vitamin D 10 μg.
Vitamin E –
Vitamin B1 1 mg.
Vitamin B2 1.6 mg.
Niacin 18 mg.
Vitamin B6 –
Vitamin B12 –
Folic acid –
Pantothenic acid –
Biotin –

[1]Recommended in the NACNE report produced by the Health Education Council in 1983.

USA Official recommended daily amounts unless otherwise stated.

Food Facts
Energy 2,350 kcal.
Protein 74 g.
Total fat 75 g.[2]
Saturated fat 25 g.[2]
Polyunsaturated fat 25 g.[2]
Carbohydrate 300 g.[2]
Sugars 62 g.[2]
Fibre –

Minerals
Calcium 1,200 mg.
Iron 63 mg.
Zinc 20 mg.
Copper –
Sodium 1,942 mg. (5 g. salt)[2]
Potassium –
Magnesium 450 mg.
Phosphorus 1,200 mg.

Vitamins
Vitamin A 1,000 μg.
Vitamin C 80 mg.
Vitamin D 11.25 μg.
Vitamin E 10 mg.
Vitamin B1 1.45 mg.
Vitamin B2 1.55 mg.
Niacin 15.5 mg.
Vitamin B6 2.6 mg.
Vitamin B12 4 μg.
Folic acid 800 μg.
Pantothenic acid –
Biotin –

[2]Recommended in a report called Dietary Goals for the United States, produced by the U.S. Senate Committee on nutrition in 1977.

Breastfeeding women

UK Official recommended daily amounts unless otherwise stated.

Food Facts
Energy 2,750 kcal.
Protein 69 g.
Total fat 88 g.[1]
Saturated fat 29 g.[1]
Polyunsaturated fat 14 g.[1]
Carbohydrate 366 g.[1]
Sugars 50 g.[1]
Fibre 30 g.[1]

Minerals
Calcium 1,200 mg.
Iron 15 mg.
Zinc –
Copper –
Sodium 3,496 mg. (9 g. salt)[1]
Potassium –
Magnesium –
Phosphorus –

Vitamins
Vitamin A 1,200 μg.
Vitamin C 60 mg.
Vitamin D 10 μg.
Vitamin E –
Vitamin B1 1.1 mg.
Vitamin B2 1.8 mg.
Niacin 21 mg.
Vitamin B6 –
Vitamin B12 –
Folic acid –
Pantothenic acid –
Biotin –

[1]Recommended in the NACNE report produced by the Health Education Council in 1983.

USA Official recommended daily amounts unless otherwise stated.

Food Facts
Energy 2,550 kcal.
Protein 64 g.
Total fat 82 g.[2]
Saturated fat 27 g.[2]
Polyunsaturated fat 27 g.[2]
Carbohydrate 326 g.[2]
Sugars 68 g.[2]
Fibre –

Minerals
Calcium 1,200 mg.
Iron 63 mg.
Zinc 25 mg.
Copper –
Sodium 1,942 mg. (5 g. salt)[2]
Potassium –
Magnesium 450 mg.
Phosphorus 1,200 mg.

Vitamins
Vitamin A 1,200 μg.
Vitamin C 1,000 mg.
Vitamin D 11.25 μg.
Vitamin E 11 mg.
Vitamin B1 1.55 mg.
Vitamin B2 1.75 mg.
Niacin 18.5 mg.
Vitamin B6 2.5 mg.
Vitamin B12 4 μg.
Folic acid 500 μg.
Pantothenic acid –
Biotin –

[2]Recommended in a report called Dietary Goals for the United States, produced by the U.S. Senate Committee on nutrition in 1977.

Women aged over 55 years

UK Official recommended daily amounts unless otherwise stated.

Food Facts
Energy 1,790 kcal.
Protein 44.5 g.
Total fat 57 g.[1]
Saturated fat 19.2 g.[1]
Polyunsaturated fat 9.6 g.[1]
Carbohydrate 238 g.[1]
Sugars 50 g.[1]
Fibre 30 g.[1]

Minerals
Calcium 500 mg.
Iron 10 mg.
Zinc –
Copper –
Sodium 3,496 mg. (9 g. salt)[1]
Potassium –
Magnesium –
Phosphorus –

Vitamins
Vitamin A 750 µg.
Vitamin C 30 mg.
Vitamin D 10 µg.
Vitamin E –
Vitamin B1 0.85 mg.
Vitamin B2 1.45 mg.
Niacin 15 mg.
Vitamin B6 –
Vitamin B12 –
Folic acid –
Pantothenic acid –
Biotin –

[1]Recommended in the NACNE report produced by the Health Education Council in 1983.

USA Official recommended daily amounts unless otherwise stated.

Food Facts
Energy 1,700 kcal.
Protein 44 g.
Total fat 54 g.[2]
Saturated fat 18.2 g.[2]
Polyunsaturated fat 18.2 g.[2]
Carbohydrate 217 g.[2]
Sugars 45 g.[2]
Fibre –

Minerals
Calcium 800 mg.
Iron 10 mg.
Zinc 15 mg.
Copper –
Sodium 1,942 mg. (5 g. salt)[2]
Potassium –
Magnesium 300 mg.
Phosphorus 800 mg.

Vitamins
Vitamin A 800 µg.
Vitamin C 60 mg.
Vitamin D 5 µg.
Vitamin E 8 mg.
Vitamin B1 1 mg.
Vitamin B2 1.2 mg.
Niacin 13 mg.
Vitamin B6 2 mg.
Vitamin B12 3 µg.
Folic acid 400 µg.
Pantothenic acid –
Biotin –

[2]Recommended in a report called Dietary Goals for the United States, produced by the U.S. Senate Committee on nutrition in 1977.

Men aged 19 to 64 years

UK Official recommended daily amounts unless otherwise stated.

Food Facts

Energy 2,400 to 2,900 kcal.
Protein 66 g.
Total fat 85 g.[1]
Saturated fat 28 g.[1]
Polyunsaturated fat 14 g.[1]
Carbohydrate 352 g.[1]
Sugars 50 g.[1]
Fibre 30 g.[1]

Minerals

Calcium 500 mg.
Iron 10 mg.
Zinc –
Copper –
Sodium 3,496 mg. (9 g. salt)[1]
Potassium –
Magnesium –
Phosphorus –

Vitamins

Vitamin A 750 μg.
Vitamin C 30 mg.
Vitamin D 10 μg.
Vitamin E –
Vitamin B1 1 mg.
Vitamin B2 1.6 mg.
Niacin 18 mg.
Vitamin B6 –
Vitamin B12 –
Folic acid –
Pantothenic acid –
Biotin –

[1]Recommended in the NACNE report produced by the Health Education Council in 1983.

USA Official recommended daily amounts unless otherwise stated.

Food Facts

Energy 2,400 to 2,900 kcal.
Protein 56 g.
Total fat 83 g.[2]
Saturated fat 27 g.[2]
Polyunsaturated fat 27 g.[2]
Carbohydrate 332 g.[2]
Sugars 69 g.[2]
Fibre –

Minerals

Calcium 800 mg.
Iron 10 mg.
Zinc 15 mg.
Copper –
Sodium 1,942 mg. (5 g. salt)[2]
Potassium –
Magnesium 350 mg.
Phosphorus 800 mg.

Vitamins

Vitamin A 1,000 μg.
Vitamin C 60 mg.
Vitamin D 6.25 μg.
Vitamin E 10 mg.
Vitamin B1 1.45 mg.
Vitamin B2 1.65 mg.
Niacin 18.5 mg.
Vitamin B6 2.2 mg.
Vitamin B12 3 μg.
Folic acid 400 μg.
Pantothenic acid –
Biotin –

[2]Recommended in a report called Dietary Goals for the United States, produced by the U.S. Senate Committee on nutrition in 1977.

Men aged over 65 years

UK Official recommended daily amounts unless otherwise stated.

Food Facts

Energy 2,150 to 2,400 kcal.
Protein 57 g.
Total fat 73 g.[1]
Saturated fat 24 g.[1]
Polyunsaturated fat 12 g.[1]
Carbohydrate 303 g.[1]
Sugars 50 g.[1]
Fibre 30 g.[1]

Minerals

Calcium 500 mg.
Iron 10 mg.
Zinc –
Copper –
Sodium 3,496 mg. (9 g. salt)[1]
Potassium –
Magnesium –
Phosphorus –

Vitamins

Vitamin A 750 μg.
Vitamin C 30 mg.
Vitamin D 10 μg.
Vitamin E –
Vitamin B1 0.99 mg.
Vitamin B2 1.6 mg.
Niacin 18 mg.
Vitamin B6 –
Vitamin B12 –
Folic acid –
Pantothenic acid –
Biotin –

[1]**Recommended in the NACNE report produced by the Health Education Council in 1983.**

USA Official recommended daily amounts unless otherwise stated.

Food Facts

Energy 2,050 to 2,400 kcal.
Protein 56 g.
Total fat 71 g.[2]
Saturated fat 23 g.[2]
Polyunsaturated fat 23 g.[2]
Carbohydrate 284 g.[2]
Sugars 59 g.[2]
Fibre –

Minerals

Calcium 800 mg.
Iron 10 mg.
Zinc 15 mg.
Copper –
Sodium 1,942 mg. (5 g. salt)[2]
Potassium –
Magnesium 350 mg.
Phosphorus 800 mg.

Vitamins

Vitamin A 1,000 μg.
Vitamin C 60 mg.
Vitamin D 5 μg.
Vitamin E 10 mg.
Vitamin B1 1.2 mg.
Vitamin B2 1.4 mg.
Niacin 16 mg.
Vitamin B6 2.2 mg.
Vitamin B12 3 μg.
Folic acid 400 μg.
Pantothenic acid –
Biotin –

[2]**Recommended in a report called Dietary Goals for the United States, produced by the U.S. Senate Committee on nutrition in 1977.**

5

What's in your food

All the foods on the following pages are given in portions which you normally eat so that you can calculate what is in the food on your plate. The portions are approximate as the size of foods vary as well as the amount people consider to be a normal serving.

The weight of the foods are given in grams (g.) and ounces (oz.). There are 28 g. to one ounce. The amount of energy a food gives you is described in kilocalories (kcalories) usually known as calories. If you want to convert them into kilojoules (the metric measure of calories), multiply the kilocalories by 4.184.

There are three figures given for fat: total fat, saturated fat and polyunsaturated fat. Where the latter two figures do not equal the total fat figure, the difference is mono-unsaturated fat (see p 8).

The carbohydrate figure includes both sugars and starch, with sugars given separately below it. Fibre is not included in the carbohydrate total and is given separately. Fibre is not absorbed into the body (see p 10).

The amount of minerals in a food is given in milligrams (mg.). There are 1,000 mg. to a gram. Remember that 388 mg. of sodium is equivalent to one gram of salt. Some vitamins are given in micrograms (μg.). There are 1,000 μg. to a milligram.

The figures in this Guide have been calculated from the following sources: *McCance and Widdowson's The Composition of Foods* by Paul and Southgate (HMSO) and Supplements; *The Handbook of Clinical Dietetics* by the American Dietetic Association (Yale University Press); *Food Tables* by Bender and Bender (Oxford University Press); Nutrition Branch, Ministry of Agriculture, Fisheries and Food.

Almonds

Portion Six whole almonds.

Weight 10 g., about ⅓ oz.

Food Facts
Energy 56 kcal.
Protein 1.7 g.
Total fat 5.3 g.
Saturated fat 0.4 g.
Polyunsaturated fat 1 g.
Carbohydrate 0.4 g.
Sugars 0.4 g.
Fibre 1.4 g.

Minerals
Calcium 25 mg.
Iron 0.42 mg.
Zinc 0.31 mg.
Copper 0.01 mg.
Sodium 0.6 mg.
Potassium 86 mg.
Magnesium 26 mg.
Phosphorus 44 mg.

Vitamins
Vitamin A None.
Vitamin C None.
Vitamin D None.
Vitamin E 2 mg.
Vitamin B1 0.02 mg.
Vitamin B2 0.09 mg.
Niacin 0.47 mg.
Vitamin B6 0.01 mg.
Vitamin B12 None.
Folic acid 9.6 µg.
Pantothenic acid None.
Biotin None.

Almonds are high in calories but a few will add texture to puddings and cereals.

Apple

Portion One eating apple without core.

Weight 100 g., about 3½ oz.

Food Facts
Energy 46 kcal.
Protein 0.3 g.
Total fat None.
Saturated fat None.
Polyunsaturated fat None.
Carbohydrate 11.9 g.
Sugars 11.8 g.
Fibre 2.0 g.

Minerals
Calcium 4 mg.
Iron 0.3 mg.
Zinc 0.1 mg.
Copper 0.04 mg.
Sodium 2 mg.
Potassium 120 mg.
Magnesium 5 mg.
Phosphorus 8 mg.

Vitamins
Vitamin A 5 µg.
Vitamin C 3 mg.
Vitamin D None.
Vitamin E 0.2 mg.
Vitamin B1 0.04 mg.
Vitamin B2 0.02 mg.
Niacin 0.1 mg.
Vitamin B6 0.03 mg.
Vitamin B12 None.
Folic acid 5 µg.
Pantothenic acid 0.1 mg.
Biotin 0.3 µg.

Wash an apple and do not peel it before eating. Apples are filling without being high in calories.

Apple, baked

Portion One medium-sized without core or sugar.

Weight 180 g., about 6½ oz.

Food Facts
Energy 55 kcal.
Protein 0.5 g.
Total fat None.
Saturated fat None.
Polyunsaturated fat None.
Carbohydrate 14.4 g.
Sugars 13.9 g.
Fibre 3.6 g.

Minerals
Calcium 5.4 mg.
Iron 0.36 mg.
Zinc 0.18 mg.
Copper 0.13 mg.
Sodium 3.6 mg.
Potassium 180 mg.
Magnesium 3.6 mg.
Phosphorus 23.4 mg.

Vitamins
Vitamin A 6.3 µg.
Vitamin C 18 mg.
Vitamin D None.
Vitamin E 0.18 mg.
Vitamin B1 0.05 mg.
Vitamin B2 0.02 mg.
Niacin 0.18 mg.
Vitamin B6 0.02 mg.
Vitamin B12 None.
Folic acid 3.6 µg.
Pantothenic acid 0.1 mg.
Biotin 0.4 µg.

Instead of having apple pie try a baked apple with natural yoghurt. Jazz it up with a little dried fruit or nuts.

Apricot

Portion One fresh apricot without stone.

Weight 65 g., about 2¼ oz.

Food Facts
Energy 18 kcal.
Protein 0.4 g.
Total fat None.
Saturated fat None.
Polyunsaturated fat None.
Carbohydrate 4.4 g.
Sugars 4.4 g.
Fibre 1.4 g.

Minerals
Calcium 11 mg.
Iron 0.26 mg.
Zinc 0.06 mg.
Copper 0.08 mg.
Sodium None.
Potassium 208 mg.
Magnesium 7.8 mg.
Phosphorus 13.6 mg.

Vitamins
Vitamin A 162 µg.
Vitamin C 4.5 mg.
Vitamin D None.
Vitamin E Not known.
Vitamin B1 0.03 mg.
Vitamin B2 0.03 mg.
Niacin 0.39 mg.
Vitamin B6 0.05 mg.
Vitamin B12 None.
Folic acid 3.2 µg.
Pantothenic acid 0.2 mg.
Biotin Not known.

In the summer fresh apricots make a nice change from plums or peaches. A good snack for slimmers.

Artichoke

Portion One globe artichoke heart.
Weight 50 g., about 2 oz.

Food Facts
Energy 3.5 kcal.
Protein 0.25 g.
Total fat None.
Saturated fat None.
Polyunsaturated fat None.
Carbohydrate 0.6 g.
Sugars Not known.
Fibre Not known.

Minerals
Calcium 9.5 mg.
Iron 0.1 mg.
Zinc Not known.
Copper 0.02 mg.
Sodium 3 mg.
Potassium 70 mg.
Magnesium 6 mg.
Phosphorus 8.5 mg.

Vitamins
Vitamin A 3.3 μg.
Vitamin C 1.5 mg.
Vitamin D None.
Vitamin E Not known.
Vitamin B1 0.01 mg.
Vitamin B2 None.
Niacin 0.2 mg.
Vitamin B6 0.01 mg.
Vitamin B12 None.
Folic acid 6.5 μg.
Pantothenic acid 0.04 mg.
Biotin 0.9 μg.

As artichoke hearts are so low in calories they make good starters. Try to make a low fat dressing for them.

Asparagus

Portion Five spears.
Weight 125 g., about 5 oz.

Food Facts
Energy 22 kcal.
Protein 4.2 g.
Total fat None.
Saturated fat None.
Polyunsaturated fat None.
Carbohydrate 1.4 g.
Sugars 1.4 g.
Fibre 1.9 g.

Minerals
Calcium 32.5 mg.
Iron 1.12 mg.
Zinc 0.37 mg.
Copper 0.25 mg.
Sodium 2.5 mg.
Potassium 300 mg.
Magnesium 12.5 mg.
Phosphorus 106 mg.

Vitamins
Vitamin A 104 μg.
Vitamin C 25 mg.
Vitamin D None.
Vitamin E 3.12 mg.
Vitamin B1 0.12 mg.
Vitamin B2 0.1 mg.
Niacin 1.75 mg.
Vitamin B6 0.05 mg.
Vitamin B12 None.
Folic acid 37.5 μg.
Pantothenic acid 0.2 mg.
Biotin 0.5 μg.

Asparagus is very high in many minerals and vitamins. In season it turns an ordinary meal into something special.

Aubergine

Portion Half including skin cooked without added fat.

Weight 130 g., about 4½ oz.

Food Facts

Energy 18 kcal.
Protein 0.9 g.
Total fat None.
Saturated fat None.
Polyunsaturated fat None.
Carbohydrate 4 g.
Sugars 3.8 g.
Fibre 3.2 g.

Minerals

Calcium 13 mg.
Iron 0.52 mg.
Zinc Not known.
Copper 0.1 mg.
Sodium 3.9 mg.
Potassium 312 mg.
Magnesium 13 mg.
Phosphorus 15.6 mg.

Vitamins

Vitamin A None.
Vitamin C 6.5 mg.
Vitamin D None.
Vitamin E Not known.
Vitamin B1 0.06 mg.
Vitamin B2 0.04 mg.
Niacin 1.17 mg.
Vitamin B6 0.1 mg.
Vitamin B12 None.
Folic acid 26 µg.
Pantothenic acid 0.3 mg.
Biotin Not known.

Aubergine is very low in calories but unfortunately people fry it. Try baking it in the oven stuffed with meat, beans or lentils.

Avocado Pear

Portion Half an avocado pear without stone.

Weight 75 g., about 2¾ oz.

Food Facts

Energy 167 kcal.
Protein 3.1 g.
Total fat 16.6 g.
Saturated fat 1.9 g.
Polyunsaturated fat 1.4 g.
Carbohydrate 1.3 g.
Sugars 1.3 g.
Fibre 1.5 g.

Minerals

Calcium 11.2 mg.
Iron 1.12 mg.
Zinc 0.32 mg.
Copper 0.16 mg.
Sodium 1.5 mg.
Potassium 300 mg.
Magnesium 21.7 mg.
Phosphorus 23.2 mg.

Vitamins

Vitamin A 12.4 µg.
Vitamin C 11.2 mg.
Vitamin D Not known.
Vitamin E 2.4 mg.
Vitamin B1 0.07 mg.
Vitamin B2 0.07 mg.
Niacin 1.35 mg.
Vitamin B6 0.31 mg.
Vitamin B12 None.
Folic acid 49.5 µg.
Pantothenic acid 0.8 mg.
Biotin 2.4 µg.

The high calorie and fat content of avocado pears makes them unsuitable for people trying to lose weight.

Baked beans

Portion Half a medium sized tin.

Weight 225 g., about 8 oz.

Food Facts
Energy 144 kcal.
Protein 11.5 g.
Total fat 1.1 g.
Saturated fat Not known.
Polyunsaturated fat Not known.
Carbohydrate 23.1 g.
Sugars 11.7 g.
Fibre 16.4 g.

Minerals
Calcium 101 mg.
Iron 3.15 mg.
Zinc 1.57 mg.
Copper 0.47 mg.
Sodium 1,080 mg.
Potassium 675 mg.
Magnesium 69.7 mg.
Phosphorus 204 mg.

Vitamins
Vitamin A None.
Vitamin C None.
Vitamin D None.
Vitamin E 1.35 mg.
Vitamin B1 0.16 mg.
Vitamin B2 0.11 mg.
Niacin 2.92 mg.
Vitamin B6 0.27 mg.
Vitamin B12 None.
Folic acid 65.2 μg.
Pantothenic acid Not known.
Biotin Not known.

Baked beans are a very good source of fibre and protein but try to buy ones which contain less sugar and salt.

Banana

Portion One medium-sized without skin.

Weight 120 g., about 4¼ oz.

Food Facts
Energy 94 kcal.
Protein 1.3 g.
Total fat 0.4 g.
Saturated fat Not known.
Polyunsaturated fat Not known.
Carbohydrate 23 g.
Sugars 19.4 g.
Fibre 4.1 g.

Minerals
Calcium 8.4 mg.
Iron 0.48 mg.
Zinc 0.24 mg.
Copper 0.19 mg.
Sodium 1.2 mg.
Potassium 420 mg.
Magnesium 50.4 mg.
Phosphorus 33.6 mg.

Vitamins
Vitamin A 40.2 μg.
Vitamin C 12 mg.
Vitamin D None.
Vitamin E 0.24 mg.
Vitamin B1 0.05 mg.
Vitamin B2 0.08 mg.
Niacin 0.96 mg.
Vitamin B6 0.61 mg.
Vitamin B12 None.
Folic acid 26.4 μg.
Pantothenic acid 0.3 mg.
Biotin Not known.

Bananas are filling and high in fibre. They also contain twice as many calories as other fruits, so slimmers beware.

Beansprouts

Portion Two tablespoons.

Weight 70 g., about 2½ oz.

Food Facts

Energy 6 kcal.
Protein 1.1 g.
Total fat None.
Saturated fat None.
Polyunsaturated fat None.
Carbohydrate 0.6 g.
Sugars 0.3 g.
Fibre 2.1 g.

Minerals

Calcium 9.1 mg.
Iron 0.7 mg.
Zinc 0.56 mg.
Copper 0.06 mg.
Sodium 56 mg.
Potassium 25 mg.
Magnesium 7 mg.
Phosphorus 14 mg.

Vitamins

Vitamin A None.
Vitamin C 0.7 mg.
Vitamin D None.
Vitamin E Not known.
Vitamin B1 0.01 mg.
Vitamin B2 0.02 mg.
Niacin 0.35 mg.
Vitamin B6 0.02 mg.
Vitamin B12 None.
Folic acid 8.4 μg.
Pantothenic acid Not known.
Biotin Not known.

Try raw beansprouts in salads or add to stir-fried vegetables cooked in a small amount of oil.

Beetroot

Portion One small whole beetroot.

Weight 35 g., about 1¼ oz.

Food Facts

Energy 15 kcal.
Protein 0.6 g.
Total fat None.
Saturated fat None.
Polyunsaturated fat None.
Carbohydrate 3.5 g.
Sugars 3.5 g.
Fibre 0.9 g.

Minerals

Calcium 10.5 mg.
Iron 0.14 mg.
Zinc 0.14 mg.
Copper 0.03 mg.
Sodium 22.4 mg.
Potassium 122.5 mg.
Magnesium 5.9 mg.
Phosphorus 12.6 mg.

Vitamins

Vitamin A None.
Vitamin C 1.75 mg.
Vitamin D None.
Vitamin E None.
Vitamin B1 0.01 mg.
Vitamin B2 0.01 mg.
Niacin 0.14 mg.
Vitamin B6 0.01 mg.
Vitamin B12 None.
Folic acid 17.5 μg.
Pantothenic acid None.
Biotin None.

Although beetroot is a starchy vegetable, a few slices in a salad will add colour but not many calories.

Blackberries

Portion Eighteen blackberries.

Weight 90 g., about 3 oz.

Food Facts
Energy 26 kcal.
Protein 1.2 g.
Total fat None.
Saturated fat None.
Polyunsaturated fat None.
Carbohydrate 5.8 g.
Sugars 5.8 g.
Fibre 6.6 g.

Minerals
Calcium 56.7 mg.
Iron 0.8 mg.
Zinc Not known.
Copper 0.11 mg.
Sodium 3.6 mg.
Potassium 189 mg.
Magnesium 27 mg.
Phosphorus 21.6 mg.

Vitamins
Vitamin A 30 µg.
Vitamin C 18 mg.
Vitamin D None.
Vitamin E 0.73 mg.
Vitamin B1 0.03 mg.
Vitamin B2 0.04 mg.
Niacin 0.54 mg.
Vitamin B6 0.04 mg.
Vitamin B12 None.
Folic acid Not known.
Pantothenic acid 0.2 mg.
Biotin 0.4 µg.

Blackberries are not only low in calories, but very high in fibre. Use them to make fruit salad and crumbles more interesting.

Blackcurrants

Portion One heaped tablespoon, stewed, no sugar.

Weight 75 g., about 3 oz.

Food Facts
Energy 18 kcal.
Protein 0.6 g.
Total fat None.
Saturated fat None.
Polyunsaturated fat None.
Carbohydrate 4.2 g.
Sugars 4.2 g.
Fibre 5.5 g.

Minerals
Calcium 38 mg.
Iron 0.82 mg.
Zinc Not known.
Copper 0.09 mg.
Sodium 2.2 mg.
Potassium 240 mg.
Magnesium 12 mg.
Phosphorus 27.7 mg.

Vitamins
Vitamin A 21.4 µg.
Vitamin C 112 mg.
Vitamin D None.
Vitamin E 0.67 mg.
Vitamin B1 0.02 mg.
Vitamin B2 0.04 mg.
Niacin 0.3 mg.
Vitamin B6 0.04 mg.
Vitamin B12 None.
Folic acid Not known.
Pantothenic acid 0.2 mg.
Biotin 1.6 µg.

When cooking blackcurrants don't add too much sugar. A tart sauce makes an ideal topping for puddings. Full of vitamin C.

Brazil nuts

Portion Three brazil nuts.

Weight 10 g., about ⅓ oz.

Food Facts
Energy 61 kcal.
Protein 1.2 g.
Total fat 6.1 g.
Saturated fat 1.57 g.
Polyunsaturated fat 2.3 g.
Carbohydrate 0.4 g.
Sugars 0.2 g.
Fibre 0.9 g.

Minerals
Calcium 18 mg.
Iron 0.28 mg.
Zinc 0.42 mg.
Copper 0.11 mg.
Sodium 0.2 mg.
Potassium 76 mg.
Magnesium 41 mg.
Phosphorus 59 mg.

Vitamins
Vitamin A None.
Vitamin C None.
Vitamin D None.
Vitamin E 0.65 mg.
Vitamin B1 0.1 mg.
Vitamin B2 0.01 mg.
Niacin 0.42 mg.
Vitamin B6 0.02 mg.
Vitamin B12 None.
Folic acid 0.4 µg.
Pantothenic acid None.
Biotin Not known.

Many muesli-type cereals are high in calories because they contain a lot of dried fruit and nuts such as brazil nuts.

Broad beans

Portion Two tablespoons, cooked.

Weight 120 g., about 4 oz.

Food Facts
Energy 57 kcal.
Protein 4.9 g.
Total fat 0.7 g.
Saturated fat Not known.
Polyunsaturated fat Not known.
Carbohydrate 8.5 g.
Sugars 0.7 g.
Fibre 5 g.

Minerals
Calcium 25.2 mg.
Iron 1.2 mg.
Zinc Not known.
Copper 0.52 mg.
Sodium 24 mg.
Potassium 276 mg.
Magnesium 33.6 mg.
Phosphorus 118.8 mg.

Vitamins
Vitamin A 49.8 µg.
Vitamin C 18 mg.
Vitamin D None.
Vitamin E None.
Vitamin B1 0.12 mg.
Vitamin B2 0.05 mg.
Niacin 4.44 mg.
Vitamin B6 Not known.
Vitamin B12 None.
Folic acid Not known.
Pantothenic acid 4.6 mg.
Biotin 2.5 µg.

Try using cooked or tinned broad beans in salads. In the summer fresh broad beans make a pleasant change from peas.

Broccoli

Portion One boiled spear.

Weight 45 g., about 1½ oz.

Food Facts
Energy 8 kcal.
Protein 1.4 g.
Total fat None.
Saturated fat None.
Polyunsaturated fat None.
Carbohydrate 0.7 g.
Sugars 0.7 g.
Fibre 1.8 g.

Minerals
Calcium 34.2 mg.
Iron 0.45 mg.
Zinc 0.18 mg.
Copper 0.04 mg.
Sodium 2.7 mg.
Potassium 99 mg.
Magnesium 5.4 mg.
Phosphorus 27 mg.

Vitamins
Vitamin A 187 μg.
Vitamin C 15.3 mg.
Vitamin D None.
Vitamin E 0.49 mg.
Vitamin B1 0.03 mg.
Vitamin B2 0.09 mg.
Niacin 0.54 mg.
Vitamin B6 0.06 mg.
Vitamin B12 None.
Folic acid 49.5 μg.
Pantothenic acid 0.3 mg.
Biotin 0.1 μg.

Broccoli is easily overcooked so try steaming it or cooking in a microwave oven.

Brussels sprouts

Portion Average serving of nine prepared boiled sprouts.
Weight 120 g., about 4¼ oz.

Food Facts
Energy 21 kcal.
Protein 3.4 g.
Total fat None.
Saturated fat None.
Polyunsaturated fat None.
Carbohydrate 2 g.
Sugars 1.9 g.
Fibre 3.5 g.

Minerals
Calcium 30 mg.
Iron 0.6 mg.
Zinc 0.48 mg.
Copper 0.06 mg.
Sodium 2.4 mg.
Potassium 288 mg.
Magnesium 15.6 mg.
Phosphorus 61.2 mg.

Vitamins
Vitamin A 79.8 μg.
Vitamin C 48 mg.
Vitamin D None.
Vitamin E 1.08 mg.
Vitamin B1 0.07 mg.
Vitamin B2 0.12 mg.
Niacin 1.08 mg.
Vitamin B6 0.2 mg.
Vitamin B12 None.
Folic acid 104 μg.
Pantothenic acid 0.3 mg.
Biotin 0.4 μg.

Brussels sprouts have an abundance of vitamins. Try to conserve them by storing away from the light and steaming them.

Cabbage, red raw

Portion One sixth of a small raw cabbage.

Weight 90 g., about 3 oz.

Food Facts

Energy 18 kcal.
Protein 1.5 g.
Total fat None.
Saturated fat None.
Polyunsaturated fat None.
Carbohydrate 3.1 g.
Sugars 3.1 g.
Fibre 3 g.

Minerals

Calcium 47 mg.
Iron 0.5 mg.
Zinc 0.27 mg.
Copper 0.08 mg.
Sodium 28 mg.
Potassium 270 mg.
Magnesium 15.3 mg.
Phosphorus 28.8 mg.

Vitamins

Vitamin A 2.9 μg.
Vitamin C 49 mg.
Vitamin D None.
Vitamin E 0.18 mg.
Vitamin B1 0.05 mg.
Vitamin B2 0.04 mg.
Niacin 0.27 mg.
Vitamin B6 0.18 mg.
Vitamin B12 None.
Folic acid 81 μg.
Pantothenic acid 0.28 mg.
Biotin 0.09 μg.

Red cabbage makes a colourful change. Try to eat it raw in salads as it is high in vitamin C.

Cabbage, white cooked

Portion One sixth of a small boiled cabbage.

Weight 90 g., about 3 oz.

Food Facts

Energy 13 kcal.
Protein 1.5 g.
Total fat None.
Saturated fat None.
Polyunsaturated fat None.
Carbohydrate 2.1 g.
Sugars 2 g.
Fibre 2.5 g.

Minerals

Calcium 34.2 mg.
Iron 0.36 mg.
Zinc 0.18 mg.
Copper 0.03 mg.
Sodium 3.6 mg.
Potassium 144 mg.
Magnesium 7.2 mg.
Phosphorus 30 mg.

Vitamins

Vitamin A 45 μg.
Vitamin C 18 mg.
Vitamin D None.
Vitamin E 0.18 mg.
Vitamin B1 0.03 mg.
Vitamin B2 0.03 mg.
Niacin 0.45 mg.
Vitamin B6 0.09 mg.
Vitamin B12 None.
Folic acid 31.5 μg.
Pantothenic acid 0.1 mg.
Biotin None.

Cook white cabbage in a very small amount of water and serve while it is still crisp as nutrients are lost through cooking.

Carrot, raw

Portion One medium sized raw carrot.

Weight 120 g., about 4¼ oz.

Food Facts
Energy 27 kcal.
Protein 0.8 g.
Total fat None.
Saturated fat None.
Polyunsaturated fat None.
Carbohydrate 6.5 g.
Sugars 6.5 g.
Fibre 3.5 g.

Minerals
Calcium 57.6 mg.
Iron 0.72 mg.
Zinc 0.48 mg.
Copper 0.1 mg.
Sodium 114 mg.
Potassium 264 mg.
Magnesium 14.4 mg.
Phosphorus 25.2 mg.

Vitamins
Vitamin A 2,400 μg.
Vitamin C 7.2 mg.
Vitamin D None.
Vitamin E 0.6 mg.
Vitamin B1 0.07 mg.
Vitamin B2 0.06 mg.
Niacin 0.84 mg.
Vitamin B6 0.18 mg.
Vitamin B12 None.
Folic acid 18 μg.
Pantothenic acid 0.3 mg.
Biotin 0.7 μg.

If you are trying to lose weight, keep some scrubbed raw carrots handy to nibble on inbetween meals.

Carrot, boiled

Portion One medium sized boiled carrot.

Weight 130 g., about 4½ oz.

Food Facts
Energy 25 kcal.
Protein 0.78 g.
Total fat None.
Saturated fat None.
Polyunsaturated fat None.
Carbohydrate 5.6 g.
Sugars 5.4 g.
Fibre 4 g.

Minerals
Calcium 48 mg.
Iron 0.52 mg.
Zinc 0.39 mg.
Copper 0.1 mg.
Sodium 65 mg.
Potassium 113 mg.
Magnesium 7.8 mg.
Phosphorus 22 mg.

Vitamins
Vitamin A 2,600 μg.
Vitamin C 5.2 mg.
Vitamin D None.
Vitamin E 0.65 mg.
Vitamin B1 0.06 mg.
Vitamin B2 0.05 mg.
Niacin 0.52 mg.
Vitamin B6 0.11 mg.
Vitamin B12 None.
Folic acid 10.4 μg.
Pantothenic acid 0.23 mg.
Biotin 0.52 μg.

Carrots contain a lot of vitamin A. Steamed carrots taste better than boiled ones.

Cashew nuts

Portion One small bag, about 24 unsalted nuts.

Weight 40 g., about 1½ oz.

Food Facts
Energy 224 kcal.
Protein 6.8 g.
Total fat 18.2 g.
Saturated fat 3.6 g.
Polyunsaturated fat 2.9 g.
Carbohydrate 11.1 g.
Sugars Not known.
Fibre 0.5 g.

Minerals
Calcium 15.2 mg.
Iron 1.5 mg.
Zinc Not known.
Copper Not known.
Sodium 6 mg.
Potassium 185 mg.
Magnesium 106 mg.
Phosphorus Not known.

Vitamins
Vitamin A 4 μg.
Vitamin C None.
Vitamin D None.
Vitamin E Not known.
Vitamin B1 0.17 mg.
Vitamin B2 0.1 mg.
Niacin 0.72 mg.
Vitamin B6 Not known.
Vitamin B12 None.
Folic acid 27.2 μg.
Pantothenic acid Not known.
Biotin Not known.

Because of their high protein content, cashew and other nuts are useful in vegetarian dishes with pulses and cereals.

Cauliflower

Portion One serving of eight cauliflower florets.

Weight 80 g., about 2¾ oz.

Food Facts
Energy 7 kcal.
Protein 1.3 g.
Total fat None.
Saturated fat None.
Polyunsaturated fat None.
Carbohydrate 0.6 g.
Sugars 0.6 g.
Fibre 1.4 g.

Minerals
Calcium 14.4 mg.
Iron 0.32 mg.
Zinc 0.16 mg.
Copper 0.02 mg.
Sodium 3.2 mg.
Potassium 144 mg.
Magnesium 6.4 mg.
Phosphorus 25.6 mg.

Vitamins
Vitamin A 4 μg.
Vitamin C 16 mg.
Vitamin D None.
Vitamin E 0.08 mg.
Vitamin B1 0.05 mg.
Vitamin B2 0.05 mg.
Niacin 0.64 mg.
Vitamin B6 0.1 mg.
Vitamin B12 None.
Folic acid 39.2 μg.
Pantothenic acid 0.3 mg.
Biotin 0.8 μg.

Cauliflower is a good very low calorie vegetable to cook or eat raw in salads. Try to include as much of the stalk as possible.

Celery

Portion One stick.

Weight 45 g., about 1½ oz.

Food Facts
Energy 3 kcal.
Protein 0.4 g.
Total fat None.
Saturated fat None.
Polyunsaturated fat None.
Carbohydrate 0.6 g.
Sugars 0.5 g.
Fibre 0.8 g.

Minerals
Calcium 23.4 mg.
Iron 0.27 mg.
Zinc 0.04 mg.
Copper 0.05 mg.
Sodium 63 mg.
Potassium 126 mg.
Magnesium 4.5 mg.
Phosphorus 14.4 mg.

Vitamins
Vitamin A None.
Vitamin C 3.15 mg.
Vitamin D None.
Vitamin E 0.09 mg.
Vitamin B1 0.01 mg.
Vitamin B2 0.01 mg.
Niacin 0.13 mg.
Vitamin B6 0.04 mg.
Vitamin B12 None.
Folic acid 5.4 μg.
Pantothenic acid 0.18 mg.
Biotin 0.4 μg.

Celery is one of the best natural slimming aids. Try a stick spread thinly with cottage cheese to stave off hunger pangs.

Cherries

Portion Six cherries without stones.

Weight 60 g., about 2 oz.

Food Facts
Energy 28 kcal.
Protein 0.4 g.
Total fat None.
Saturated fat None.
Polyunsaturated fat None.
Carbohydrate 7.1 g.
Sugars 7.1 g.
Fibre 1 g.

Minerals
Calcium 9.6 mg.
Iron 0.24 mg.
Zinc 0.06 mg.
Copper 0.04 mg.
Sodium 1.8 mg.
Potassium 168 mg.
Magnesium 6 mg.
Phosphorus 10.2 mg.

Vitamins
Vitamin A 12 μg.
Vitamin C 3 mg.
Vitamin D None.
Vitamin E 0.06 mg.
Vitamin B1 0.03 mg.
Vitamin B2 0.04 mg.
Niacin 0.24 mg.
Vitamin B6 0.03 mg.
Vitamin B12 None.
Folic acid 4.8 μg.
Pantothenic acid 0.2 mg.
Biotin 0.2 μg.

Treat yourself to some cherries instead of sweets. A quarter of a pound will only contain as many calories as an apple.

Chestnuts

Portion Five chestnuts peeled.

Weight 50 g., about 2 oz.

Food Facts

Energy 85 kcal.
Protein 1 g.
Total fat 1.35 g.
Saturated fat 0.24 g.
Polyunsaturated fat 0.56 g.
Carbohydrate 18.3 g.
Sugars 3.5 g.
Fibre 3.4 g.

Minerals

Calcium 23 mg.
Iron 0.45 mg.
Zinc Not known.
Copper 0.11 mg.
Sodium 5.5 mg.
Potassium 250 mg.
Magnesium 16.5 mg.
Phosphorus 37 mg.

Vitamins

Vitamin A None.
Vitamin C None.
Vitamin D None.
Vitamin E 0.25 mg.
Vitamin B1 0.1 mg.
Vitamin B2 0.11 mg.
Niacin 0.1 mg.
Vitamin B6 0.16 mg.
Vitamin B12 None.
Folic acid Not known.
Pantothenic acid 0.23 mg.
Biotin 0.65 μg.

Chestnuts are lower in calories than other nuts. Try using them in stuffings in place of sausage meat.

Chickpeas

Portion Two to three tablespoons cooked.

Weight 200 g., about 7 oz.

Food Facts

Energy 288 kcal.
Protein 16 g.
Total fat 6.6 g.
Saturated fat Not known.
Polyunsaturated fat Not known.
Carbohydrate 44 g.
Sugars 10.4 g.
Fibre 12 g.

Minerals

Calcium 128 mg.
Iron 6.2 mg.
Zinc 2.8 mg.
Copper 0.66 mg.
Sodium 1,700 mg.
Potassium 800 mg.
Magnesium 134 mg.
Phosphorus 260 mg.

Vitamins

Vitamin A 174 μg.
Vitamin C 6 mg.
Vitamin D 0.1 μg.
Vitamin E None.
Vitamin B1 0.28 mg.
Vitamin B2 0.1 mg.
Niacin 3.2 mg.
Vitamin B6 Not known.
Vitamin B12 None.
Folic acid 74 μg.
Pantothenic acid Not known.
Biotin Not known.

Chickpeas are very high in fibre but also high in calories so try to eat them as part of your main meal and not as a vegetable.

Chicory

Portion One head of chicory.

Weight 105 g., about 3¾ oz.

Food Facts
Energy 9 kcal.
Protein 0.8 g.
Total fat None.
Saturated fat None.
Polyunsaturated fat None.
Carbohydrate 1.5 g.
Sugars Not known.
Fibre Not known.

Minerals
Calcium 18.9 mg.
Iron 0.73 mg.
Zinc 0.21 mg.
Copper 0.14 mg.
Sodium 7.3 mg.
Potassium 189 mg.
Magnesium 13.6 mg.
Phosphorus 22 mg.

Vitamins
Vitamin A None.
Vitamin C 4.2 mg.
Vitamin D None.
Vitamin E Not known.
Vitamin B1 0.05 mg.
Vitamin B2 0.05 mg.
Niacin 0.52 mg.
Vitamin B6 0.05 mg.
Vitamin B12 None.
Folic acid 54 μg.
Pantothenic acid Not known.
Biotin Not known.

Chicory makes an ideal low calorie addition to salads.

Chillies

Portion One raw chilli.

Weight 5 g., about ⅙ oz.

Food Facts
Energy 5.8 kcal.
Protein 0.3 g.
Total fat 0.07 g.
Saturated fat Not known.
Polyunsaturated fat Not known.
Carbohydrate 0.4 g.
Sugars Not known.
Fibre Not known.

Minerals
Calcium 4.3 mg.
Iron 0.18 mg.
Zinc 0.01 mg.
Copper None.
Sodium 1.15 mg.
Potassium 64 mg.
Magnesium 0.9 mg.
Phosphorus Not known.

Vitamins
Vitamin A 55 μg.
Vitamin C 4.8 mg.
Vitamin D None.
Vitamin E Not known.
Vitamin B1 0.01 mg.
Vitamin B2 0.02 mg.
Niacin 0.12 mg.
Vitamin B6 Not known.
Vitamin B12 None.
Folic acid 0.8 μg.
Pantothenic acid Not known.
Biotin Not known.

A small amount of fresh chilli is much more potent than chilli powder. The seeds are the hottest part.

Chinese leaves

Portion One large leaf.

Weight 40 g., about 1½ oz.

Food Facts
Energy 10.4 kcal.
Protein 1.4 g.
Total fat 0.04 g.
Saturated fat Not known.
Polyunsaturated fat Not known.
Carbohydrate 1.4 g.
Sugars Not known.
Fibre Not known.

Minerals
Calcium 61.6 mg.
Iron 1.16 mg.
Zinc Not known.
Copper 0.14 mg.
Sodium Not known.
Potassium Not known.
Magnesium 64 mg.
Phosphorus Not known.

Vitamins
Vitamin A 436 μg.
Vitamin C 9.2 mg.
Vitamin D None.
Vitamin E Not known.
Vitamin B1 0.01 mg.
Vitamin B2 0.08 mg.
Niacin 0.28 mg.
Vitamin B6 Not known.
Vitamin B12 None.
Folic acid 34 μg.
Pantothenic acid Not known.
Biotin Not known.

Chinese leaves contain many vitamins and minerals and make a welcome change from lettuce, particularly in the winter.

Coleslaw

Portion One tablespoon of shop-bought coleslaw.

Weight 75 g., about 2¾ oz.

Food Facts
Energy 60 kcal.
Protein 1.4 g.
Total fat 4.1 g.
Saturated fat Not known.
Polyunsaturated fat Not known.
Carbohydrate 4.6 g.
Sugars Not known.
Fibre 1.6 g.

Minerals
Calcium 31.5 mg.
Iron 0.37 mg.
Zinc 0.15 mg.
Copper 0.03 mg.
Sodium 130 mg.
Potassium 180 mg.
Magnesium 11.2 mg.
Phosphorus 35.2 mg.

Vitamins
Vitamin A None.
Vitamin C 24 mg.
Vitamin D None.
Vitamin E None.
Vitamin B1 0.04 mg.
Vitamin B2 0.03 mg.
Niacin 0.37 mg.
Vitamin B6 0.1 mg.
Vitamin B12 None.
Folic acid 15.7 μg.
Pantothenic acid 0.1 mg.
Biotin None.

If you are watching your weight, use lemon juice instead of mayonnaise in your home-made coleslaw.

Courgettes

Portion One courgette cooked without fat.

Weight 100 g., about 3½ oz.

Food Facts
Energy 25 kcal.
Protein 1.6 g.
Total fat 0.4 g.
Saturated fat Not known.
Polyunsaturated fat Not known.
Carbohydrate 4.5 g.
Sugars Not known.
Fibre Not known.

Minerals
Calcium 30 mg.
Iron 2.4 mg.
Zinc Not known.
Copper Not known.
Sodium 1 mg.
Potassium 202 mg.
Magnesium 6 mg.
Phosphorus Not known.

Vitamins
Vitamin A 58 μg.
Vitamin C 16 mg.
Vitamin D None.
Vitamin E Not known.
Vitamin B1 0.05 mg.
Vitamin B2 0.09 mg.
Niacin 0.4 mg.
Vitamin B6 Not known.
Vitamin B12 None.
Folic acid 48 μg.
Pantothenic acid Not known.
Biotin Not known.

Courgettes absorb a lot of fat so try steaming them or make a vegetable dish by cooking them with onions or tomatoes.

Cucumber

Portion One sixth, about 2 in. long, including skin.

Weight 80 g., about 2¾ oz.

Food Facts
Energy 8 kcal.
Protein 0.5 g.
Total fat 0.1 g.
Saturated fat Not known.
Polyunsaturated fat Not known.
Carbohydrate 1.4 g.
Sugars 1.4 g.
Fibre 0.3 g.

Minerals
Calcium 18.4 mg.
Iron 0.24 mg.
Zinc 0.08 mg.
Copper 0.07 mg.
Sodium 10.4 mg.
Potassium 112 mg.
Magnesium 7.2 mg.
Phosphorus 19.2 mg.

Vitamins
Vitamin A None.
Vitamin C 6.4 mg.
Vitamin D None.
Vitamin E None.
Vitamin B1 0.03 mg.
Vitamin B2 0.03 mg.
Niacin 0.24 mg.
Vitamin B6 0.03 mg.
Vitamin B12 None.
Folic acid 12.8 μg.
Pantothenic acid 0.2 mg.
Biotin 0.3 μg.

Try grated cucumber in plain yoghurt as a low calorie alternative to coleslaw.

Dates, dried

Portion One dried date.

Weight 15 g., about ½ oz.

Food Facts
Energy 37 kcal.
Protein 0.3 g.
Total fat None.
Saturated fat None.
Polyunsaturated fat None.
Carbohydrate 9.6 g.
Sugars 9.6 g.
Fibre 1.3 g.

Minerals
Calcium 10.2 mg.
Iron 0.24 mg.
Zinc 0.04 mg.
Copper 0.03 mg.
Sodium 0.7 mg.
Potassium 112 mg.
Magnesium 8.8 mg.
Phosphorus 9.6 mg.

Vitamins
Vitamin A 1.3 μg.
Vitamin C None.
Vitamin D None.
Vitamin E Not known.
Vitamin B1 0.01 mg.
Vitamin B2 0.01 mg.
Niacin 0.43 mg.
Vitamin B6 0.02 mg.
Vitamin B12 None.
Folic acid 3.1 μg.
Pantothenic acid 0.1 mg.
Biotin Not known.

Dried dates often have added syrup and it is easy to eat a lot of them. Avoid them if you are trying to lose weight.

Figs, dried

Portion One dried fig.

Weight 20 g., about ⅔ oz.

Food Facts
Energy 42 kcal.
Protein 0.7 g.
Total fat None.
Saturated fat None.
Polyunsaturated fat None.
Carbohydrate 10.6 g.
Sugars 10.6 g.
Fibre 3.7 g.

Minerals
Calcium 56 mg.
Iron 0.84 mg.
Zinc 0.18 mg.
Copper 0.05 mg.
Sodium 17.4 mg.
Potassium 202 mg.
Magnesium 18.4 mg.
Phosphorus 18.4 mg.

Vitamins
Vitamin A 1.7 μg.
Vitamin C None.
Vitamin D None.
Vitamin E Not known.
Vitamin B1 0.02 mg.
Vitamin B2 0.02 mg.
Niacin 0.44 mg.
Vitamin B6 0.04 mg.
Vitamin B12 None.
Folic acid 1.8 μg.
Pantothenic acid 0.1 mg.
Biotin Not known.

Half of the weight of a dried fig comes from sugars, so although they are high in fibre and iron, they are also high in calories.

Figs, fresh

Portion One fresh fig.

Weight 55 g., about 2 oz.

Food Facts
Energy 22.5 kcal.
Protein 0.7 g.
Total fat None.
Saturated fat None.
Polyunsaturated fat None.
Carbohydrate 5.2 g.
Sugars 5.2 g.
Fibre 1.4 g.

Minerals
Calcium 18.7 mg.
Iron 0.22 mg.
Zinc 0.16 mg.
Copper 0.03 mg.
Sodium 1.1 mg.
Potassium 1.48 mg.
Magnesium 11 mg.
Phosphorus 17.6 mg.

Vitamins
Vitamin A 45 µg.
Vitamin C 1.1 mg.
Vitamin D None.
Vitamin E Not known.
Vitamin B1 0.03 mg.
Vitamin B2 0.02 mg.
Niacin 0.22 mg.
Vitamin B6 0.06 mg.
Vitamin B12 None.
Folic acid Not known.
Pantothenic acid 0.16 mg.
Biotin Not known.

Fresh figs make a good dessert. Either eat whole or cut up into fruit salads.

Garlic

Portion One peeled clove.

Weight 5 g., about ⅕ oz.

Food Facts
Energy 5.8 kcal.
Protein 0.17 g.
Total fat 0.01 g.
Saturated fat Not known.
Polyunsaturated fat Not known.
Carbohydrate 1.3 g.
Sugars Not known.
Fibre Not known.

Minerals
Calcium 0.9 mg.
Iron 0.07 mg.
Zinc 0.04 mg.
Copper Not known.
Sodium 0.9 mg.
Potassium 18.6 mg.
Magnesium 0.4 mg.
Phosphorus Not known.

Vitamins
Vitamin A None.
Vitamin C 0.5 mg.
Vitamin D None.
Vitamin E Not known.
Vitamin B1 0.01 mg.
Vitamin B2 None.
Niacin 0.02 mg.
Vitamin B6 Not known.
Vitamin B12 None.
Folic acid 0.3 µg.
Pantothenic acid Not known.
Biotin Not known.

Garlic can be used to flavour low calorie dishes and also helps to make foods taste better if you are adding less salt.

Gherkin

Portion One pickled gherkin about three inches long.
Weight 30 g., about 1 oz.

Food Facts
Energy 3.3 kcal.
Protein 0.3 g.
Total fat Not known.
Saturated fat Not known.
Polyunsaturated fat Not known.
Carbohydrate 0.54 g.
Sugars Not known.
Fibre 0.33 g.

Minerals
Calcium 7.5 mg.
Iron 0.09 mg.
Zinc 0.06 mg.
Copper 0.04 mg.
Sodium 3.3 mg.
Potassium 67 mg.
Magnesium 4.5 mg.
Phosphorus Not known.

Vitamins
Vitamin A 6.8 μg.
Vitamin C 3.3 mg.
Vitamin D None.
Vitamin E Not known.
Vitamin B1 None.
Vitamin B2 0.01 mg.
Niacin 0.06 mg.
Vitamin B6 Not known.
Vitamin B12 None.
Folic acid 5.4 μg.
Pantothenic acid Not known.
Biotin Not known.

Gherkins can be added in small amounts to cottage cheese to flavour it. They also make sandwiches taste better.

Gooseberries

Portion A quarter of a pound stewed with sugar.
Weight 112 g., about 4 oz.

Food Facts
Energy 15 kcal.
Protein 1 g.
Total fat None.
Saturated fat None.
Polyunsaturated fat None.
Carbohydrate 3.2 g.
Sugars 3.2 g.
Fibre 3 g.

Minerals
Calcium 26.9 mg.
Iron 0.34 mg.
Zinc 0.11 mg.
Copper 0.12 mg.
Sodium 2.2 mg.
Potassium 201 mg.
Magnesium 6.7 mg.
Phosphorus 32.5 mg.

Vitamins
Vitamin A 28 μg.
Vitamin C 34 mg.
Vitamin D None.
Vitamin E 0.34 mg.
Vitamin B1 0.03 mg.
Vitamin B2 0.03 mg.
Niacin 0.56 mg.
Vitamin B6 0.02 mg.
Vitamin B12 None.
Folic acid Not known.
Pantothenic acid 0.1 mg.
Biotin 0.4 μg.

Make a low calorie gooseberry fool with a little sugar or artificial sweetener and skimmed milk.

Grapefruit

Portion Half a grapefruit, flesh only.
Weight 80 g., about 2¾ oz.

Food Facts
Energy 17 kcal.
Protein 0.5 g.
Total fat None.
Saturated fat None.
Polyunsaturated fat None.
Carbohydrate 4.2 g.
Sugars 4.2 g.
Fibre 0.5 g.

Minerals
Calcium 13.6 mg.
Iron 0.24 mg.
Zinc 0.08 mg.
Copper 0.05 mg.
Sodium 0.8 mg.
Potassium 184 mg.
Magnesium 8 mg.
Phosphorus 12.8 mg.

Vitamins
Vitamin A None.
Vitamin C 32 mg.
Vitamin D None.
Vitamin E 0.24 mg.
Vitamin B1 0.04 mg.
Vitamin B2 0.02 mg.
Niacin 0.24 mg.
Vitamin B6 0.02 mg.
Vitamin B12 None.
Folic acid 9.6 μg.
Pantothenic acid 0.2 mg.
Biotin 0.8 μg.

Although grapefruits do not have any magical slimming powers, they are very low in calories and contain a lot of vitamin C.

Grapes, black

Portion About 20 peeled grapes.
Weight 112 g., about 4 oz.

Food Facts
Energy 57 kcal.
Protein 0.56 g.
Total fat None.
Saturated fat None.
Polyunsaturated fat None.
Carbohydrate 14.5 g.
Sugars 14.5 g.
Fibre 0.3 g.

Minerals
Calcium 4.4 mg.
Iron 0.3 mg.
Zinc 0.11 mg.
Copper 0.07 mg.
Sodium 1.1 mg.
Potassium 302 mg.
Magnesium 3.3 mg.
Phosphorus 15.6 mg.

Vitamins
Vitamin A None.
Vitamin C 3.36 mg.
Vitamin D None.
Vitamin E Not known.
Vitamin B1 0.03 mg.
Vitamin B2 0.02 mg.
Niacin 0.22 mg.
Vitamin B6 0.08 mg.
Vitamin B12 None.
Folic acid 5.6 μg.
Pantothenic acid 0.04 mg.
Biotin 0.22 μg.

Black grapes contain slightly fewer calories than white grapes and compared to other fruits provide little fibre.

Grapes, white

Portion About 20 unpeeled grapes.
Weight 112 g., about 4 oz.

Food Facts
Energy 67 kcal.
Protein 0.7 g.
Total fat None.
Saturated fat None.
Polyunsaturated fat None.
Carbohydrate 17.1 g.
Sugars 17.1 g.
Fibre 1 g.

Minerals
Calcium 20.2 mg.
Iron 0.34 mg.
Zinc 0.11 mg.
Copper 0.11 mg.
Sodium 2.2 mg.
Potassium 268 mg.
Magnesium 6.7 mg.
Phosphorus 23.5 mg.

Vitamins
Vitamin A None.
Vitamin C 4.48 mg.
Vitamin D None.
Vitamin E Not known.
Vitamin B1 0.04 mg.
Vitamin B2 0.02 mg.
Niacin 0.34 mg.
Vitamin B6 0.11 mg.
Vitamin B12 None.
Folic acid 6.7 µg.
Pantothenic acid 0.05 mg.
Biotin 0.3 µg.

A few grapes added to a winter fruit salad will make it more interesting and colourful. Not a fruit for slimmers.

Hazel nuts

Portion One handful, about ten hazelnuts.
Weight 10 g., about ⅓ oz.

Food Facts
Energy 38 kcal.
Protein 0.8 g.
Total fat 3.6 g.
Saturated fat 0.2 g.
Polyunsaturated fat 0.3 g.
Carbohydrate 0.7 g.
Sugars 0.5 g.
Fibre 0.6 g.

Minerals
Calcium 4.4 mg.
Iron 0.11 mg.
Zinc 0.24 mg.
Copper 0.02 mg.
Sodium 0.1 mg.
Potassium 35 mg.
Magnesium 5.6 mg.
Phosphorus 23 mg.

Vitamins
Vitamin A None.
Vitamin C None.
Vitamin D None.
Vitamin E 2.1 mg.
Vitamin B1 0.04 mg.
Vitamin B2 Not known.
Niacin 0.31 mg.
Vitamin B6 0.05 mg.
Vitamin B12 None.
Folic acid 7.2 µg.
Pantothenic acid 0.1 mg.
Biotin Not known.

Hazel nuts are lower in calories than other nuts but should still be used sparingly if you wish to lose weight.

Kidney beans

Portion About two cooked tablespoons. Dried weight 2 oz.
Weight 160 g., about 5½ oz.

Food Facts
Energy 152 kcal.
Protein 12.4 g.
Total fat 1 g.
Saturated fat Not known.
Polyunsaturated fat Not known.
Carbohydrate 25.2 g.
Sugars 1.7 g.
Fibre 1.4 g.

Minerals
Calcium 78 mg.
Iron 3.75 mg.
Zinc 1.57 mg.
Copper 0.34 mg.
Sodium 22.4 mg.
Potassium 649 mg.
Magnesium 100 mg.
Phosphorus 229 mg.

Vitamins
Vitamin A None.
Vitamin C None.
Vitamin D None.
Vitamin E Not known.
Vitamin B1 0.3 mg.
Vitamin B2 0.1 mg.
Niacin 3.08 mg.
Vitamin B6 0.25 mg.
Vitamin B12 None.
Folic acid 72 µg.
Pantothenic acid 0.3 mg.
Biotin Not known.

Use less meat by replacing it with kidney beans. This will keep the protein content of the dish the same but reduce the fat.

Kiwi fruit

Portion One medium sized.
Weight 60 g., about 2 oz.

Food Facts
Energy 32 kcal.
Protein 0.7 g.
Total fat 0.4 g.
Saturated fat 0.11 g.
Polyunsaturated fat 0.14 g.
Carbohydrate 7.0 g.
Sugars 7.0 g.
Fibre 1.4 g.

Minerals
Calcium 15 mg.
Iron 0.2 mg.
Zinc 0.12 mg.
Copper 0.12 mg.
Sodium 1.2 mg.
Potassium 216 mg.
Magnesium 12 mg.
Phosphorus 24 mg.

Vitamins
Vitamin A 11 µg.
Vitamin C 60 mg.
Vitamin D None.
Vitamin E 0.1 mg. (estimated)
Vitamin B1 0.01 mg.
Vitamin B2 0.01 mg.
Niacin 0.15 mg.
Vitamin B6 0.06 mg. (estimated)
Vitamin B12 None.
Folic acid 14 µg. (estimated)
Pantothenic acid Not known.
Biotin Not known.

One kiwi fruit contains almost the same amount of vitamin C as one orange. If you don't like citrus fruit, it is a very nutritious alternative.

Leeks

Portion One medium sized boiled leek.

Weight 160 g., about 5¾ oz.

Food Facts

Energy 38 kcal.
Protein 2.9 g.
Total fat None.
Saturated fat None.
Polyunsaturated fat None.
Carbohydrate 7.4 g.
Sugars 7.4 g.
Fibre 6.2 g.

Minerals

Calcium 97.6 mg.
Iron 3.2 mg.
Zinc 0.16 mg.
Copper 0.14 mg.
Sodium 9.6 mg.
Potassium 448 mg.
Magnesium 20.8 mg.
Phosphorus 44.8 mg.

Vitamins

Vitamin A 10.4 μg.
Vitamin C 24 mg.
Vitamin D None.
Vitamin E 1.28 mg.
Vitamin B1 0.11 mg.
Vitamin B2 0.05 mg.
Niacin 1.12 mg.
Vitamin B6 0.24 mg.
Vitamin B12 None.
Folic acid Not known.
Pantothenic acid 0.2 mg.
Biotin 1.6 μg.

Leeks can make very good salad vegetables crisply cooked and also well flavoured home-made soups.

Lemon

Portion One average sized including peel.

Weight 100 g., about 3½ oz.

Food Facts

Energy 15 kcal.
Protein 0.8 g.
Total fat None.
Saturated fat None.
Polyunsaturated fat None.
Carbohydrate 3.2 g.
Sugars 3.2 g.
Fibre 5.2 g.

Minerals

Calcium 110 mg.
Iron 0.4 mg.
Zinc 0.1 mg.
Copper 0.26 mg.
Sodium 6 mg.
Potassium 160 mg.
Magnesium 12 mg.
Phosphorus 21 mg.

Vitamins

Vitamin A None.
Vitamin C 80 mg.
Vitamin D None.
Vitamin E Not known.
Vitamin B1 0.05 mg.
Vitamin B2 0.04 mg.
Niacin 0.3 mg.
Vitamin B6 0.11 mg.
Vitamin B12 None.
Folic acid 12 μg.
Pantothenic acid 0.2 mg.
Biotin 0.5 μg.

A slice of lemon will add taste and vitamin C squeezed onto foods and drinks.

Lentils

Portion One-third cup of raw lentils boiled (raw weight 2 oz.).

Weight 120 g., about 4¼ oz.

Food Facts

Energy 118 kcal.
Protein 9.1 g.
Total fat 0.6 g.
Saturated fat Not known.
Polyunsaturated fat Not known.
Carbohydrate 20.4 g.
Sugars 0.9 g.
Fibre 4.4 g.

Minerals

Calcium 15.6 mg.
Iron 2.8 mg.
Zinc 1.2 mg.
Copper 0.22 mg.
Sodium 14.4 mg.
Potassium 252 mg.
Magnesium 30 mg.
Phosphorus 92 mg.

Vitamins

Vitamin A 3.9 μg.
Vitamin C None.
Vitamin D None.
Vitamin E Not known.
Vitamin B1 0.13 mg.
Vitamin B2 0.04 mg.
Niacin 0.4 mg.
Vitamin B6 0.13 mg.
Vitamin B12 None.
Folic acid 6 μg.
Pantothenic acid 0.3 mg.
Biotin Not known.

Add lentils to stews and use less meat. Lentils also make good main course soups.

Lettuce

Portion One serving of four small leaves.

Weight 20 g., about ⅔ oz.

Food Facts

Energy 2 kcal.
Protein 0.2 g.
Total fat 0.1 g.
Saturated fat Not known.
Polyunsaturated fat Not known.
Carbohydrate 0.2 g.
Sugars 0.2 g.
Fibre 0.3 g.

Minerals

Calcium 4.6 mg.
Iron 0.18 mg.
Zinc 0.04 mg.
Copper 0.01 mg.
Sodium 1.8 mg.
Potassium 48 mg.
Magnesium 1.6 mg.
Phosphorus 5.4 mg.

Vitamins

Vitamin A 33.3 μg.
Vitamin C 3 mg.
Vitamin D None.
Vitamin E 0.1 mg.
Vitamin B1 0.01 mg.
Vitamin B2 0.02 mg.
Niacin 0.08 mg.
Vitamin B6 0.01 mg.
Vitamin B12 None.
Folic acid 6.8 μg.
Pantothenic acid None.
Biotin 0.1 μg.

Put lettuce in sandwiches to add bulk without adding calories.

Lychees

Portion One tinned lychee without skin or stone.

Weight 13 g., about ½ oz.

Food Facts
Energy 8 kcal.
Protein 0.1 g.
Total fat None.
Saturated fat None.
Polyunsaturated fat None.
Carbohydrate 2.3 g.
Sugars 2.3 g.
Fibre 0.1 g.

Minerals
Calcium 0.5 mg.
Iron 0.09 mg.
Zinc 0.03 mg.
Copper 0.01 mg.
Sodium 0.3 mg.
Potassium 9.8 mg.
Magnesium 0.8 mg.
Phosphorus 1.6 mg.

Vitamins
Vitamin A None.
Vitamin C 1.04 mg.
Vitamin D None.
Vitamin E Not known.
Vitamin B1 None.
Vitamin B2 None.
Niacin 0.04 mg.
Vitamin B6 Not known.
Vitamin B12 None.
Folic acid Not known.
Pantothenic acid Not known.
Biotin Not known.

Tinned or fresh lychees will enhance fruit salads and other puddings.

Mandarin oranges

Portion Eighteen segments from a tin.

Weight 80 g., about 3 oz.

Food Facts
Energy 44 kcal.
Protein 0.5 g.
Total fat None.
Saturated fat None.
Polyunsaturated fat None.
Carbohydrate 11.4 g.
Sugars 11.4 g.
Fibre 0.2 g.

Minerals
Calcium 14.4 mg.
Iron 0.32 mg.
Zinc 0.32 mg.
Copper 0.04 mg.
Sodium 7.2 mg.
Potassium 70.4 mg.
Magnesium 7.2 mg.
Phosphorus 9.6 mg.

Vitamins
Vitamin A 40 μg.
Vitamin C 11.2 mg.
Vitamin D None.
Vitamin E None.
Vitamin B1 0.06 mg.
Vitamin B2 0.02 mg.
Niacin 0.24 mg.
Vitamin B6 0.02 mg.
Vitamin B12 None.
Folic acid 6.4 μg.
Pantothenic acid 0.12 mg.
Biotin 0.64 μg.

Try to get mandarin oranges canned in natural juice without sugar added. Use them to decorate trifles and cheesecakes.

Mango

Portion One medium-sized, fresh, raw mango without stone or peel.
Weight 160 g., about 5¾ oz.

Food Facts
Energy 94 kcal.
Protein 0.8 g.
Total fat None.
Saturated fat None.
Polyunsaturated fat None.
Carbohydrate 24.5 g.
Sugars 24.5 g.
Fibre 2.4 g.

Minerals
Calcium 16 mg.
Iron 0.8 mg.
Zinc 0.75 mg.
Copper 0.19 mg.
Sodium 11.2 mg.
Potassium 304 mg.
Magnesium 28.8 mg.
Phosphorus 20.8 mg.

Vitamins
Vitamin A 320 μg.
Vitamin C 48 mg.
Vitamin D None.
Vitamin E Not known.
Vitamin B1 0.05 mg.
Vitamin B2 0.06 mg.
Niacin 0.64 mg.
Vitamin B6 Not known.
Vitamin B12 None.
Folic acid 0.3 μg.
Pantothenic acid 0.25 mg.
Biotin Not known.

The yellow colour of the mango makes it high in vitamin A. It also contains a lot of vitamin C.

Marrow

Portion One average serving.
Weight 224 g., about 8 oz.

Food Facts
Energy 15 kcal.
Protein 0.9 g.
Total fat None.
Saturated fat None.
Polyunsaturated fat None.
Carbohydrate 3.1 g.
Sugars 2.9 g.
Fibre 1.3 g.

Minerals
Calcium 31.4 mg.
Iron 0.45 mg.
Zinc 0.45 mg.
Copper 0.07 mg.
Sodium 2.2 mg.
Potassium 188 mg.
Magnesium 15.7 mg.
Phosphorus 29.1 mg.

Vitamins
Vitamin A 11.2 μg.
Vitamin C 4.48 mg.
Vitamin D None.
Vitamin E None.
Vitamin B1 None.
Vitamin B2 None.
Niacin 0.67 mg.
Vitamin B6 0.07 mg.
Vitamin B12 None.
Folic acid 13.4 μg.
Pantothenic acid 0.2 mg.
Biotin Not known.

Try stuffing marrow with beans or lentils instead of meat.

Melon, canteloupe

Portion One slice without skin.

Weight 180 g., about 6½ oz.

Food Facts
Energy 43 kcal.
Protein 1.8 g.
Total fat None.
Saturated fat None.
Polyunsaturated fat None.
Carbohydrate 9.5 g.
Sugars 9.5 g.
Fibre 1.8 g.

Minerals
Calcium 34 mg.
Iron 1.4 mg.
Zinc 0.18 mg.
Copper 0.07 mg.
Sodium 25 mg.
Potassium 576 mg.
Magnesium 36 mg.
Phosphorus 54 mg.

Vitamins
Vitamin A 599 µg.
Vitamin C 45 mg.
Vitamin D None.
Vitamin E 0.18 mg.
Vitamin B1 0.09 mg.
Vitamin B2 0.05 mg.
Niacin 0.9 mg.
Vitamin B6 0.12 mg.
Vitamin B12 None.
Folic acid 54 µg.
Pantothenic acid 0.41 mg.
Biotin Not known.

Compared to other melons, the canteloupe contains a lot of vitamin A due to its yellow-coloured flesh. A delicious starter.

Melon, honey dew

Portion One slice without skin.

Weight 180 g., about 6½ oz.

Food Facts
Energy 37 kcal.
Protein 1.1 g.
Total fat None.
Saturated fat None.
Polyunsaturated fat None.
Carbohydrate 9 g.
Sugars 9 g.
Fibre 1.6 g.

Minerals
Calcium 25.2 mg.
Iron 0.36 mg.
Zinc 0.18 mg.
Copper 0.07 mg.
Sodium 36 mg.
Potassium 396 mg.
Magnesium 23.4 mg.
Phosphorus 16.2 mg.

Vitamins
Vitamin A 29.7 µg.
Vitamin C 45 mg.
Vitamin D None.
Vitamin E 0.18 mg.
Vitamin B1 0.09 mg.
Vitamin B2 0.05 mg.
Niacin 0.9 mg.
Vitamin B6 0.13 mg.
Vitamin B12 None.
Folic acid 54 µg.
Pantothenic acid 0.4 mg.
Biotin Not known.

Honey dew and canteloupe melons are both high in vitamin C and folic acid. Try mixing different kinds of melon together for an unusual desert.

Mixed vegetables

Portion One tablespoon from frozen packet, boiled.

Weight 80 g., about 2¾ oz.

Food Facts

Energy 33 kcal.
Protein 1.7 g.
Total fat 0.2 g.
Saturated fat Not known.
Polyunsaturated fat Not known.
Carbohydrate 6.7 g.
Sugars 2.4 g.
Fibre 2.9 g.

Minerals

Calcium 20.8 mg.
Iron 0.56 mg.
Zinc 0.32 mg.
Copper 0.08 mg.
Sodium 64 mg.
Potassium 124 mg.
Magnesium 10.4 mg.
Phosphorus 32.8 mg.

Vitamins

Vitamin A 533 μg.
Vitamin C 6.4 mg.
Vitamin D None.
Vitamin E 0.16 mg.
Vitamin B1 0.06 mg.
Vitamin B2 0.05 mg.
Niacin 0.8 mg.
Vitamin B6 0.08 mg.
Vitamin B12 None.
Folic acid 17.6 μg.
Pantothenic acid 0.16 mg.
Biotin None.

Frozen mixed vegetables are useful if you are in a hurry.

Mushrooms, raw

Portion One average serving raw.

Weight 60 g., about 2 oz.

Food Facts

Energy 7 kcal.
Protein 1.1 g.
Total fat 0.4 g.
Saturated fat Not known.
Polyunsaturated fat Not known.
Carbohydrate None.
Sugars None.
Fibre 1.5 g.

Minerals

Calcium 1.8 mg.
Iron 0.6 mg.
Zinc 0.06 mg.
Copper 0.38 mg.
Sodium 5.4 mg.
Potassium 282 mg.
Magnesium 7.8 mg.
Phosphorus 84 mg.

Vitamins

Vitamin A None.
Vitamin C 1.8 mg.
Vitamin D None.
Vitamin E None.
Vitamin B1 0.06 mg.
Vitamin B2 0.24 mg.
Niacin 2.76 mg.
Vitamin B6 0.06 mg.
Vitamin B12 None.
Folic acid 13.8 μg.
Pantothenic acid 1.2 mg.
Biotin Not known.

Try adding raw mushrooms to salads making sure that they are well washed.

Mushrooms, fried

Portion One average serving fried in butter.

Weight 44 g., about 1½ oz.

Food Facts
Energy 92 kcal.
Protein 0.96 g.
Total fat 0.98 g.
Saturated fat 4.7 g.
Polyunsaturated fat 0.22 g.
Carbohydrate None.
Sugars None.
Fibre 1.76 g.

Minerals
Calcium 1.76 mg.
Iron 0.57 mg.
Zinc 0.04 mg.
Copper 0.34 mg.
Sodium 4.8 mg.
Potassium 250 mg.
Magnesium 7 mg.
Phosphorus 74 mg.

Vitamins
Vitamin A None.
Vitamin C 0.44 mg.
Vitamin D None.
Vitamin E None.
Vitamin B1 0.03 mg.
Vitamin B2 0.15 mg.
Niacin 1.54 mg.
Vitamin B6 0.02 mg.
Vitamin B12 None.
Folic acid 8.8 µg.
Pantothenic acid 0.61 mg.
Biotin Not known.

Cook mushrooms in other ways, such as poaching, so they retain their low calorie value. Mushrooms weigh less after cooking.

Mustard and cress

Portion One quarter of a punnet.

Weight 10 g., about ⅓ oz.

Food Facts
Energy 1 kcal.
Protein 0.2 g.
Total fat None.
Saturated fat None.
Polyunsaturated fat None.
Carbohydrate 0.1 g.
Sugars 0.1 g.
Fibre 0.4 g.

Minerals
Calcium 6.6 mg.
Iron 0.1 mg.
Zinc Not known.
Copper 0.01 mg.
Sodium 1.9 mg.
Potassium 34 mg.
Magnesium 2.7 mg.
Phosphorus 6.6 mg.

Vitamins
Vitamin A 50 µg.
Vitamin C 4 mg.
Vitamin D None.
Vitamin E 0.07 mg.
Vitamin B1 Not known.
Vitamin B2 Not known.
Niacin 0.03 mg.
Vitamin B6 Not known.
Vitamin B12 None.
Folic acid Not known.
Pantothenic acid Not known.
Biotin Not known.

Useful as a low calorie garnish or additional sandwich filling.

Nectarine

Portion One medium sized without stone.

Weight 110 g., about 4 oz.

Food Facts

Energy 55 kcal.
Protein 1 g.
Total fat None.
Saturated fat None.
Polyunsaturated fat None.
Carbohydrate 13.6 g.
Sugars 13.6 g.
Fibre 2.6 g.

Minerals

Calcium 4.4 mg.
Iron 0.55 mg.
Zinc 0.11 mg.
Copper 0.07 mg.
Sodium 9.9 mg.
Potassium 297 mg.
Magnesium 14.3 mg.
Phosphorus 26.4 mg.

Vitamins

Vitamin A 550 μg.
Vitamin C 8.8 mg.
Vitamin D None.
Vitamin E Not known.
Vitamin B1 0.02 mg.
Vitamin B2 0.05 mg.
Niacin 1.21 mg.
Vitamin B6 0.02 mg.
Vitamin B12 None.
Folic acid 5.5 μg.
Pantothenic acid 0.2 mg.
Biotin Not known.

Nectarines make a pleasant change from peaches. Be sure to eat the skin to increase your fibre intake.

Okra

Portion Twelve medium sized raw okra about 2 in. long.

Weight 60 g., about 2 oz.

Food Facts

Energy 10 kcal.
Protein 1.2 g.
Total fat None.
Saturated fat None.
Polyunsaturated fat None.
Carbohydrate 1.4 g.
Sugars 1.4 g.
Fibre 1.9 g.

Minerals

Calcium 42 mg.
Iron 0.6 mg.
Zinc Not known.
Copper 0.11 mg.
Sodium 4.2 mg.
Potassium 114 mg.
Magnesium 36 mg.
Phosphorus 36 mg.

Vitamins

Vitamin A 9 μg.
Vitamin C 15 mg.
Vitamin D None.
Vitamin E Not known.
Vitamin B1 0.06 mg.
Vitamin B2 0.06 mg.
Niacin 0.78 mg.
Vitamin B6 0.05 mg.
Vitamin B12 None.
Folic acid 60 μg.
Pantothenic acid 0.2 mg.
Biotin Not known.

Not a traditional English vegetable but becoming increasingly available. Fry using only a little oil.

Olives

Portion Five black olives without stones in brine.

Weight 15 g., about ½ oz.

Food Facts

Energy 15 kcal.
Protein 0.1 g.
Total fat 1.6 g.
Saturated fat Not known.
Polyunsaturated fat Not known.
Carbohydrate None.
Sugars None.
Fibre 0.7 g.

Minerals

Calcium 9.1 mg.
Iron 0.15 mg.
Zinc 0.04 mg.
Copper 0.03 mg.
Sodium 337 mg.
Potassium 13.6 mg.
Magnesium 3.3 mg.
Phosphorus 2.5 mg.

Vitamins

Vitamin A 4.5 μg.
Vitamin C None.
Vitamin D None.
Vitamin E Not known.
Vitamin B1 None.
Vitamin B2 None.
Niacin 0.1 mg.
Vitamin B6 None.
Vitamin B12 None.
Folic acid Not known.
Pantothenic acid None.
Biotin None.

Olives are quite low in calories so add them to salads and rice dishes for a different taste.

Onion, raw

Portion One average sized raw onion.

Weight 90 g., about 3 oz.

Food Facts

Energy 20 kcal.
Protein 0.8 g.
Total fat None.
Saturated fat None.
Polyunsaturated fat None.
Carbohydrate 4.7 g.
Sugars 4.7 g.
Fibre 1.2 g.

Minerals

Calcium 27.9 mg.
Iron 0.27 mg.
Zinc 0.09 mg.
Copper 0.07 mg.
Sodium 9 mg.
Potassium 126 mg.
Magnesium 7.2 mg.
Phosphorus 27 mg.

Vitamins

Vitamin A None.
Vitamin C 9 mg.
Vitamin D None.
Vitamin E Not known.
Vitamin B1 0.03 mg.
Vitamin B2 0.04 mg.
Niacin 0.36 mg.
Vitamin B6 0.09 mg.
Vitamin B12 None.
Folic acid 14.4 μg.
Pantothenic acid 0.1 mg.
Biotin 0.8 μg.

Add small amounts to cottage cheese or salads to increase the flavour.

Onion, fried

Portion One average sized onion fried in butter.
Weight 57 g., about 2 oz.

Food Facts
Energy 196 kcal.
Protein 1.02 g.
Total fat 18.9 g.
Saturated fat 9.3 g.
Polyunsaturated fat 0.38 g.
Carbohydrate 5.7 g.
Sugars 5.7 g.
Fibre Not known.

Minerals
Calcium 34.5 mg.
Iron 0.33 mg.
Zinc 0.04 mg.
Copper 0.09 mg.
Sodium 11.4 mg.
Potassium 153 mg.
Magnesium 8.5 mg.
Phosphorus 33.6 mg.

Vitamins
Vitamin A None.
Vitamin C Not known.
Vitamin D None.
Vitamin E None.
Vitamin B1 Not known.
Vitamin B2 Not known.
Niacin 0.22 mg.
Vitamin B6 Not known.
Vitamin B12 None.
Folic acid Not known.
Pantothenic acid Not known.
Biotin Not known.

Contrast the calorie value and other nutrients with that of raw onion. Most vegetables are low in calories until you fry them.

Orange

Portion One medium sized, peeled.
Weight 140 g., about 5 oz.

Food Facts
Energy 49 kcal.
Protein 1.1 g.
Total fat None.
Saturated fat None.
Polyunsaturated fat None.
Carbohydrate 11.9 g.
Sugars 11.9 g.
Fibre 2.8 g.

Minerals
Calcium 57.4 mg.
Iron 0.42 mg.
Zinc 0.28 mg.
Copper 0.1 mg.
Sodium 4.2 mg.
Potassium 280 mg.
Magnesium 18.2 mg.
Phosphorus 33.6 mg.

Vitamins
Vitamin A 11.9 μg.
Vitamin C 70 mg.
Vitamin D None.
Vitamin E 0.28 mg.
Vitamin B1 0.14 mg.
Vitamin B2 0.04 mg.
Niacin 0.42 mg.
Vitamin B6 0.08 mg.
Vitamin B12 None.
Folic acid 51.8 μg.
Pantothenic acid 0.3 mg.
Biotin 1.4 μg.

One orange contains twice the UK recommended daily intake of vitamin C.

Parsley

Portion One sprig.

Weight 2 g., about 1/14 oz.

Food Facts
Energy None.
Protein 0.1 g.
Total fat None.
Saturated fat None.
Polyunsaturated fat None.
Carbohydrate None.
Sugars None.
Fibre 0.2 g.

Minerals
Calcium 6.6 mg.
Iron 0.16 mg.
Zinc 0.02 mg.
Copper 0.01 mg.
Sodium 0.7 mg.
Potassium 21.6 mg.
Magnesium 1 mg.
Phosphorus 2.6 mg.

Vitamins
Vitamin A 23 μg.
Vitamin C 3 mg.
Vitamin D None.
Vitamin E 0.04 mg.
Vitamin B1 None.
Vitamin B2 0.01 mg.
Niacin 0.04 mg.
Vitamin B6 None.
Vitamin B12 None.
Folic acid Not known.
Pantothenic acid None.
Biotin None.

Parsley adds colour to many dishes and flavour to sauces.

Parsnips

Portion One medium sized, peeled.
Weight 120 g., about 4 oz.

Food Facts
Energy 67 kcal.
Protein 1.6 g.
Total fat None.
Saturated fat None.
Polyunsaturated fat None.
Carbohydrate 16.2 g.
Sugars 3.2 g.
Fibre 3 g.

Minerals
Calcium 43.2 mg.
Iron 0.6 mg.
Zinc 0.12 mg.
Copper 0.12 mg.
Sodium 4.8 mg.
Potassium 348 mg.
Magnesium 15.6 mg.
Phosphorus 38.4 mg.

Vitamins
Vitamin A None.
Vitamin C 12 mg.
Vitamin D None.
Vitamin E 1.2 mg.
Vitamin B1 0.08 mg.
Vitamin B2 0.07 mg.
Niacin 1.08 mg.
Vitamin B6 0.07 mg.
Vitamin B12 None.
Folic acid 36 μg.
Pantothenic acid 0.4 mg.
Biotin None.

Instead of roasting your parsnips try steaming them next time you have a Sunday roast.

Passion Fruit

Portion One average sized, flesh and seeds only.
Weight 15 g., about ½ oz.

Food Facts
Energy 5 kcal.
Protein 0.4 g.
Total fat None.
Saturated fat None.
Polyunsaturated fat None.
Carbohydrate 0.9 g.
Sugars 0.9 g.
Fibre 2.4 g.

Minerals
Calcium 2.4 mg.
Iron 0.16 mg.
Zinc Not known.
Copper 0.02 mg.
Sodium 4.2 mg.
Potassium 52.5 mg.
Magnesium 5.8 mg.
Phosphorus 8.1 mg.

Vitamins
Vitamin A 0.2 μg.
Vitamin C 3 mg.
Vitamin D None.
Vitamin E Not known.
Vitamin B1 None.
Vitamin B2 0.01 mg.
Niacin 0.28 mg.
Vitamin B6 Not known.
Vitamin B12 None.
Folic acid Not known.
Pantothenic acid Not known.
Biotin Not known.

The flesh of a passion fruit is mostly seeds so it is high in fibre. Add just one to any fruit dish for a distinctive flavour.

Peach, fresh

Portion One medium sized without stone.
Weight 110 g., about 4 oz.

Food Facts
Energy 40 kcal.
Protein 0.7 g.
Total fat None.
Saturated fat None.
Polyunsaturated fat None.
Carbohydrate 10 g.
Sugars 10 g.
Fibre 1.5 g.

Minerals
Calcium 5.5 mg.
Iron 0.44 mg.
Zinc 0.11 mg.
Copper 0.05 mg.
Sodium 3.3 mg.
Potassium 286 mg.
Magnesium 8.8 mg.
Phosphorus 20.9 mg.

Vitamins
Vitamin A 91.8 μg.
Vitamin C 8.8 mg.
Vitamin D None.
Vitamin E Not known.
Vitamin B1 0.02 mg.
Vitamin B2 0.05 mg.
Niacin 1.1 mg.
Vitamin B6 0.02 mg.
Vitamin B12 None.
Folic acid 3.3 μg.
Pantothenic acid 0.2 mg.
Biotin 0.2 μg.

In the summer, eat fresh peaches or serve chilled in medium or sweet wine with a spot of honey for extra flavour.

Peaches, tinned

Portion One small bowlful of ten slices.

Weight 105 g., about 3¾ oz.

Food Facts
Energy 91 kcal.
Protein 0.4 g.
Total fat None.
Saturated fat None.
Polyunsaturated fat None.
Carbohydrate 24 g.
Sugars 24 g.
Fibre 1 g.

Minerals
Calcium 4.2 mg.
Iron 0.42 mg.
Zinc 0.1 mg.
Copper 0.06 mg.
Sodium 1 mg.
Potassium 157 mg.
Magnesium 6.3 mg.
Phosphorus 10.5 mg.

Vitamins
Vitamin A 43.6 μg.
Vitamin C 4.2 mg.
Vitamin D None.
Vitamin E Not known.
Vitamin B1 0.01 mg.
Vitamin B2 0.02 mg.
Niacin 0.63 mg.
Vitamin B6 0.02 mg.
Vitamin B12 None.
Folic acid 3.1 μg.
Pantothenic acid 0.1 mg.
Biotin 0.2 μg.

If you eat tinned peaches regularly, try those tinned in natural juice with no added sugar. They cost a few pence more but are much tastier.

Peanuts, salted

Portion One small bag containing about 25 whole nuts.

Weight 25 g., about 1 oz.

Food Facts
Energy 142 kcal.
Protein 6.1 g.
Total fat 12.2 g.
Saturated fat 2.6 g.
Polyunsaturated fat 3.4 g.
Carbohydrate 2.1 g.
Sugars 0.8 g.
Fibre 2 g.

Minerals
Calcium 15.2 mg.
Iron 0.5 mg.
Zinc 0.75 mg.
Copper 0.07 mg.
Sodium 110 mg.
Potassium 170 mg.
Magnesium 45 mg.
Phosphorus 92 mg.

Vitamins
Vitamin A None.
Vitamin C None.
Vitamin D None.
Vitamin E 2.02 mg.
Vitamin B1 0.06 mg.
Vitamin B2 0.02 mg.
Niacin 5.32 mg.
Vitamin B6 0.1 mg.
Vitamin B12 None.
Folic acid Not known.
Pantothenic acid 0.5 mg.
Biotin Not known.

Although peanuts are high in fibre, they are also very high in calories and salt.

Peanut butter

Portion Thickly spread to cover one slice of bread.
Weight 15 g., about ½ oz.

Food Facts
Energy 93 kcal.
Protein 3.4 g.
Total fat 8.1 g.
Saturated fat 1.5 g.
Polyunsaturated fat 2 g.
Carbohydrate 2 g.
Sugars 1 g.
Fibre 1.1 g.

Minerals
Calcium 5.5 mg.
Iron 0.31 mg.
Zinc 0.45 mg.
Copper 0.1 mg.
Sodium 52.5 mg.
Potassium 105 mg.
Magnesium 27 mg.
Phosphorus 49.5 mg.

Vitamins
Vitamin A None.
Vitamin C None.
Vitamin D None.
Vitamin E 0.7 mg.
Vitamin B1 0.03 mg.
Vitamin B2 0.01 mg.
Niacin 2.98 mg.
Vitamin B6 0.07 mg.
Vitamin B12 None.
Folic acid 7.9 μg.
Pantothenic acid 0.3 mg.
Biotin Not known.

Peanut butter is very high in calories and should be used as sparingly as jam. An alternative to cheese.

Pear

Portion One medium sized without core.
Weight 150 g., about 5¼ oz.

Food Facts
Energy 61 kcal.
Protein 0.4 g.
Total fat None.
Saturated fat None.
Polyunsaturated fat None.
Carbohydrate 15.9 g.
Sugars 15.9 g.
Fibre 3.4 g.

Minerals
Calcium 12 mg.
Iron 0.3 mg.
Zinc 0.15 mg.
Copper 0.22 mg.
Sodium 3 mg.
Potassium 195 mg.
Magnesium 10.5 mg.
Phosphorus 15 mg.

Vitamins
Vitamin A 2.2 μg.
Vitamin C 4.5 mg.
Vitamin D None.
Vitamin E None.
Vitamin B1 0.04 mg.
Vitamin B2 0.04 mg.
Niacin 0.3 mg.
Vitamin B6 0.03 mg.
Vitamin B12 None.
Folic acid 16.5 μg.
Pantothenic acid 0.1 mg.
Biotin 0.1 μg.

Many people think pears are high in calories but they only contain a few more than an apple or orange and are also quite high in fibre.

Peas, frozen

Portion One average tablespoon serving, boiled.
Weight 80 g., about 2¾ oz.

Food Facts
Energy 32 kcal.
Protein 4.3 g.
Total fat 0.3 g.
Saturated fat Not known.
Polyunsaturated fat Not known.
Carbohydrate 3.4 g.
Sugars 0.8 g.
Fibre 9.6 g.

Minerals
Calcium 24.8 mg.
Iron 1.12 mg.
Zinc 0.56 mg.
Copper 0.15 mg.
Sodium 1.6 mg.
Potassium 104 mg.
Magnesium 18.4 mg.
Phosphorus 67.2 mg.

Vitamins
Vitamin A 40 μg.
Vitamin C 10.4 mg.
Vitamin D None.
Vitamin E None.
Vitamin B1 0.19 mg.
Vitamin B2 0.06 mg.
Niacin 1.92 mg.
Vitamin B6 0.06 mg.
Vitamin B12 None.
Folic acid 62.4 μg.
Pantothenic acid 0.3 mg.
Biotin 0.3 μg.

Adding peas to stews and casseroles will help to increase the fibre content.

Peas, tinned

Portion One average serving of a tablespoon.
Weight 85 g., about 3 oz.

Food Facts
Energy 39 kcal.
Protein 3.9 g.
Total fat 0.3 g.
Saturated fat Not known.
Polyunsaturated fat Not known.
Carbohydrate 5.9 g.
Sugars 3.1 g.
Fibre 5.4 g.

Minerals
Calcium 20.4 mg.
Iron 1.36 mg.
Zinc 0.59 mg.
Copper 0.14 mg.
Sodium 195 mg.
Potassium 110 mg.
Magnesium 14.4 mg.
Phosphorus 62 mg.

Vitamins
Vitamin A 42.5 μg.
Vitamin C 6.8 mg.
Vitamin D None.
Vitamin E None.
Vitamin B1 0.11 mg.
Vitamin B2 0.08 mg.
Niacin 2.38 mg.
Vitamin B6 0.05 mg.
Vitamin B12 None.
Folic acid 44.2 μg.
Pantothenic acid 0.1 mg.
Biotin 0.3 μg.

Tinned peas not only have added sugar but also contain less fibre than frozen or fresh peas.

Pepper, green

Portion Half a medium sized pepper.
Weight 80 g., about 3 oz.

Food Facts
Energy 12 kcal.
Protein 0.7 g.
Total fat 0.3 g.
Saturated fat Not known.
Polyunsaturated fat Not known.
Carbohydrate 1.8 g.
Sugars 1.8 g.
Fibre 0.7 g.

Minerals
Calcium 7.2 mg.
Iron 0.3 mg.
Zinc 0.16 mg.
Copper 0.06 mg.
Sodium 1.6 mg.
Potassium 168 mg.
Magnesium 8.8 mg.
Phosphorus 20 mg.

Vitamins
Vitamin A 26.8 μg.
Vitamin C 80 mg.
Vitamin D None.
Vitamin E 0.64 mg.
Vitamin B1 None.
Vitamin B2 0.02 mg.
Niacin 0.72 mg.
Vitamin B6 0.14 mg.
Vitamin B12 None.
Folic acid 8.8 μg.
Pantothenic acid 0.2 mg.
Biotin Not known.

Red peppers are sweeter than green so contain a few more calories. Both are nutritious and rich in vitamin C.

Pineapple, fresh

Portion One large slice fresh pineapple.
Weight 80 g., about 3 oz.

Food Facts
Energy 36 kcal.
Protein 0.4 g.
Total fat None.
Saturated fat None.
Polyunsaturated fat None.
Carbohydrate 9.28 g.
Sugars 9.28 g.
Fibre 0.96 g.

Minerals
Calcium 9.6 mg.
Iron 0.32 mg.
Zinc 0.08 mg.
Copper 0.06 mg.
Sodium 1.6 mg.
Potassium 200 mg.
Magnesium 13.6 mg.
Phosphorus 6.4 mg.

Vitamins
Vitamin A 8 μg.
Vitamin C 20 mg.
Vitamin D None.
Vitamin E Not known.
Vitamin B1 0.06 mg.
Vitamin B2 0.01 mg.
Niacin 0.16 mg.
Vitamin B6 0.07 mg.
Vitamin B12 None.
Folic acid 8.8 μg.
Pantothenic acid 0.12 mg.
Biotin None.

Fresh pineapple is much lower in calories than most tinned pineapple or pineapple juice.

Pineapple, tinned

Portion Two pineapple rings.

Weight 80 g., about 3 oz.

Food Facts
Energy 61 kcal.
Protein 0.2 g.
Total fat None.
Saturated fat None.
Polyunsaturated fat None.
Carbohydrate 16.2 g.
Sugars 16.2 g.
Fibre 0.7 g.

Minerals
Calcium 10.4 mg.
Iron 0.32 mg.
Zinc 0.06 mg.
Copper 0.04 mg.
Sodium 0.8 mg.
Potassium 75.2 mg.
Magnesium 6.4 mg.
Phosphorus 4 mg.

Vitamins
Vitamin A 5.2 μg.
Vitamin C 9.6 mg.
Vitamin D None.
Vitamin E Not known.
Vitamin B1 0.04 mg.
Vitamin B2 0.02 mg.
Niacin 0.16 mg.
Vitamin B6 0.06 mg.
Vitamin B12 None.
Folic acid 8.8 μg.
Pantothenic acid 0.1 mg.
Biotin None.

Tinned pineapple with added sugar contains half as much vitamin C as fresh pineapple and often twice as much sugar (look at the label).

Plantain

Portion One whole boiled, without skin.

Weight 140 g., about 5 oz.

Food Facts
Energy 170 kcal.
Protein 1.4 g.
Total fat 0.1 g.
Saturated fat Not known.
Polyunsaturated fat Not known.
Carbohydrate 43.5 g.
Sugars 1.3 g.
Fibre 9 g.

Minerals
Calcium 12.6 mg.
Iron 0.56 mg.
Zinc 0.28 mg.
Copper 0.14 mg.
Sodium 5.6 mg.
Potassium 4.62 mg.
Magnesium 47.6 mg.
Phosphorus 47.6 mg.

Vitamins
Vitamin A 14 μg.
Vitamin C 4.2 mg.
Vitamin D None.
Vitamin E Not known.
Vitamin B1 None.
Vitamin B2 0.01 mg.
Niacin 0.7 mg.
Vitamin B6 0.42 mg.
Vitamin B12 None.
Folic acid 25.2 μg.
Pantothenic acid 0.4 mg.
Biotin Not known.

A high fibre addition to stews and casseroles. Frying them increases the calories.

Plum

Portion One eating plum without stone.
Weight 35 g., about 1¼ oz.

Food Facts
Energy 13 kcal.
Protein 0.2 g.
Total fat None.
Saturated fat None.
Polyunsaturated fat None.
Carbohydrate 3.4 g.
Sugars 3.4 g.
Fibre 0.7 g.

Minerals
Calcium 3.8 mg.
Iron 0.14 mg.
Zinc None.
Copper 0.03 mg.
Sodium 0.7 mg.
Potassium 66.5 mg.
Magnesium 2.4 mg.
Phosphorus 5.6 mg.

Vitamins
Vitamin A 12.8 μg.
Vitamin C 1.05 mg.
Vitamin D None.
Vitamin E 0.24 mg.
Vitamin B1 0.02 mg.
Vitamin B2 0.01 mg.
Niacin 0.21 mg.
Vitamin B6 0.02 mg.
Vitamin B12 None.
Folic acid 1 μg.
Pantothenic acid 0.1 mg.
Biotin None.

Plums are low in calories and so are good to eat in between meals if you are trying to lose weight.

Potato chips

Portion One average fish and chip shop portion.
Weight 260 g., about 9¼ oz.

Food Facts
Energy 657 kcal.
Protein 9.9 g.
Total fat 28.3 g.
Saturated fat 4.6 g.
Polyunsaturated fat 13.9 g.
Carbohydrate 97 g.
Sugars Not known.
Fibre Not known.

Minerals
Calcium 36.4 mg.
Iron 2.34 mg.
Zinc 1.56 mg.
Copper 0.7 mg.
Sodium 31.2 mg.
Potassium 2,652 mg.
Magnesium 111 mg.
Phosphorus 187 mg.

Vitamins
Vitamin A None.
Vitamin C 26 mg.
Vitamin D None.
Vitamin E 0.26 mg.
Vitamin B1 0.26 mg.
Vitamin B2 0.1 mg.
Niacin 5.4 mg.
Vitamin B6 0.47 mg.
Vitamin B12 None.
Folic acid 26 μg.
Pantothenic acid 0.5 mg.
Biotin None.

Only eat chips occasionally. It is better to cook them yourself in oil that is only used a few times.

Potato crisps

Portion One small bag.

Weight 30 g., about 1 oz.

Food Facts
Energy 159 kcal.
Protein 1.9 g.
Total fat 10.8 g.
Saturated fat Not known.
Polyunsaturated fat Not known.
Carbohydrate 14.8 g.
Sugars 0.2 g.
Fibre 3.5 g.

Minerals
Calcium 11.1 mg.
Iron 0.63 mg.
Zinc 0.24 mg.
Copper 0.07 mg.
Sodium 165 mg.
Potassium 357 mg.
Magnesium 16.8 mg.
Phosphorus 39 mg.

Vitamins
Vitamin A None.
Vitamin C 5.1 mg.
Vitamin D None.
Vitamin E 1.83 mg.
Vitamin B1 0.06 mg.
Vitamin B2 0.02 mg.
Niacin 1.83 mg.
Vitamin B6 0.27 mg.
Vitamin B12 None.
Folic acid 6 μg.
Pantothenic acid Not known.
Biotin Not known.

A raw carrot provides as much fibre and a lot less calories than a bag of crisps.

Potato salad

Portion One tablespoon, fresh or tinned.

Weight 100 g., about 3½ oz.

Food Facts
Energy 133 kcal.
Protein 1.3 g.
Total fat 8.3 g.
Saturated fat Not known.
Polyunsaturated fat Not known.
Carbohydrate 14.4 g.
Sugars 4.2 g.
Fibre 0.5 g.

Minerals
Calcium 12 mg.
Iron 0.4 mg.
Zinc 0.1 mg.
Copper 0.08 mg.
Sodium 254 mg.
Potassium 189 mg.
Magnesium 14 mg.
Phosphorus 42 mg.

Vitamins
Vitamin A Not known.
Vitamin C 4 mg.
Vitamin D Not known.
Vitamin E Not known.
Vitamin B1 0.04 mg.
Vitamin B2 0.02 mg.
Niacin 0.4 mg.
Vitamin B6 0.09 mg.
Vitamin B12 None.
Folic acid 5 μg.
Pantothenic acid 0.1 mg.
Biotin None.

Try making a lower calorie, lower fat potato salad by mixing half mayonnaise with half plain yoghurt.

Potatoes, boiled

Portion Two medium sized, peeled potatoes.
Weight 200 g., about 7 oz.

Food Facts
Energy 160 kcal.
Protein 2.8 g.
Total fat 0.2 g.
Saturated fat Not known.
Polyunsaturated fat Not known.
Carbohydrate 39.4 g.
Sugars 0.8 g.
Fibre 2 g.

Minerals
Calcium 8 mg.
Iron 0.6 mg.
Zinc 0.4 mg.
Copper 0.22 mg.
Sodium 6 mg.
Potassium 660 mg.
Magnesium 30 mg.
Phosphorus 58 mg.

Vitamins
Vitamin A None.
Vitamin C 18 mg.
Vitamin D None.
Vitamin E 0.2 mg.
Vitamin B1 0.16 mg.
Vitamin B2 0.06 mg.
Niacin 2.2 mg.
Vitamin B6 0.36 mg.
Vitamin B12 None.
Folic acid 20 µg.
Pantothenic acid 0.4 mg.
Biotin None.

In the summer, boil new potatoes in their jackets for extra fibre.

Potatoes, jacket

Portion Two medium sized potatoes including skin.
Weight 260 g., about 9¼ oz.

Food Facts
Energy 221 kcal.
Protein 5.5 g.
Total fat 0.3 g.
Saturated fat Not known.
Polyunsaturated fat Not known.
Carbohydrate 52.8 g.
Sugars 1.3 g.
Fibre 5.2 g.

Minerals
Calcium 20.8 mg.
Iron 1.56 mg.
Zinc 0.52 mg.
Copper 0.39 mg.
Sodium 15.6 mg.
Potassium 1,430 mg.
Magnesium 62.4 mg.
Phosphorus 101 mg.

Vitamins
Vitamin A None.
Vitamin C 20.8 mg.
Vitamin D None.
Vitamin E 0.26 mg.
Vitamin B1 0.21 mg.
Vitamin B2 0.08 mg.
Niacin 3.9 mg.
Vitamin B6 0.36 mg.
Vitamin B12 None.
Folic acid 20.8 µg.
Pantothenic acid 0.4 mg.
Biotin None.

A nutritious and convenient snack as well as an addition to a main meal.

Potatoes, roasted

Portion Two medium sized, peeled and roasted in lard.
Weight 200 g., about 7 oz.

Food Facts

Energy 314 kcal.
Protein 5.6 g.
Total fat 9.6 g.
Saturated fat 4 g.
Polyunsaturated fat 0.8 g.
Carbohydrate 54.6 g.
Sugars Not known.
Fibre Not known.

Minerals

Calcium 20 mg.
Iron 1.4 mg.
Zinc 0.8 mg.
Copper 0.4 mg.
Sodium 18 mg.
Potassium 1,500 mg.
Magnesium 64 mg.
Phosphorus 106 mg.

Vitamins

Vitamin A None.
Vitamin C 20 mg.
Vitamin D None.
Vitamin E 0.2 mg.
Vitamin B1 0.2 mg.
Vitamin B2 0.08 mg.
Niacin 3.8 mg.
Vitamin B6 0.36 mg.
Vitamin B12 None.
Folic acid 14 µg.
Pantothenic acid 0.4 mg.
Biotin None.

For a change try a jacket potato with your Sunday roast.

Prunes

Portion Six prunes without stones stewed without sugar.
Weight 35 g., about 1¼ oz.

Food Facts

Energy 28 kcal.
Protein 0.5 g.
Total fat None.
Saturated fat None.
Polyunsaturated fat None.
Carbohydrate 7.1 g.
Sugars 7.1 g.
Fibre 2.8 g.

Minerals

Calcium 6.6 mg.
Iron 0.49 mg.
Zinc 0.11 mg.
Copper 0.03 mg.
Sodium 2.4 mg.
Potassium 154 mg.
Magnesium 4.5 mg.
Phosphorus 14.7 mg.

Vitamins

Vitamin A 29.7 µg.
Vitamin C None.
Vitamin D None.
Vitamin E Not known.
Vitamin B1 0.01 mg.
Vitamin B2 0.03 mg.
Niacin 0.35 mg.
Vitamin B6 0.03 mg.
Vitamin B12 None.
Folic acid None.
Pantothenic acid 0.1 mg.
Biotin None.

Prunes stewed without sugar are good to add to many different types of breakfast cereals.

Radishes

Portion Three medium radishes.
Weight 30 g., about 1 oz.

Food Facts
Energy 4 kcal.
Protein 0.3 g.
Total fat None.
Saturated fat None.
Polyunsaturated fat None.
Carbohydrate 0.8 g.
Sugars 0.8 g.
Fibre 0.3 g.

Minerals
Calcium 13.2 mg.
Iron 0.57 mg.
Zinc 0.03 mg.
Copper 0.04 mg.
Sodium 17.7 mg.
Potassium 72 mg.
Magnesium 3.3 mg.
Phosphorus 8.1 mg.

Vitamins
Vitamin A None.
Vitamin C 7.5 mg.
Vitamin D None.
Vitamin E None.
Vitamin B1 0.01 mg.
Vitamin B2 0.01 mg.
Niacin 0.12 mg.
Vitamin B6 0.03 mg.
Vitamin B12 None.
Folic acid 7.2 μg.
Pantothenic acid 0.1 mg.
Biotin Not known.

An attractive and colourful addition to any salad.

Raisins

Portion One handful of about thirty raisins.
Weight 15 g., about ½ oz.

Food Facts
Energy 36 kcal.
Protein 0.2 g.
Total fat None.
Saturated fat None.
Polyunsaturated fat None.
Carbohydrate 9.7 g.
Sugars 9.7 g.
Fibre 1 g.

Minerals
Calcium 9.1 mg.
Iron 0.24 mg.
Zinc 0.01 mg.
Copper 0.04 mg.
Sodium 7.8 mg.
Potassium 129 mg.
Magnesium 6.3 mg.
Phosphorus 4.9 mg.

Vitamins
Vitamin A 0.7 μg.
Vitamin C None.
Vitamin D None.
Vitamin E Not known.
Vitamin B1 0.01 mg.
Vitamin B2 0.01 mg.
Niacin 0.09 mg.
Vitamin B6 0.04 mg.
Vitamin B12 None.
Folic acid 0.6 μg.
Pantothenic acid None.
Biotin Not known.

Like other dried fruit raisins contain a lot of natural sugar. However they are an alternative to sweets for children.

Raspberries

Portion Fifteen raspberries.

Weight 75 g., about 3 oz.

Food Facts
Energy 18 kcal.
Protein 0.7 g.
Total fat None.
Saturated fat None.
Polyunsaturated fat None.
Carbohydrate 4.2 g.
Sugars 4.2 g.
Fibre 5.5 g.

Minerals
Calcium 30.7 mg.
Iron 0.9 mg.
Zinc Not known.
Copper 0.16 mg.
Sodium 2.2 mg.
Potassium 165 mg.
Magnesium 16.5 mg.
Phosphorus 21.7 mg.

Vitamins
Vitamin A 10.1 μg.
Vitamin C 18.7 mg.
Vitamin D None.
Vitamin E 0.22 mg.
Vitamin B1 0.01 mg.
Vitamin B2 0.02 mg.
Niacin 0.37 mg.
Vitamin B6 0.04 mg.
Vitamin B12 None.
Folic acid Not known.
Pantothenic acid 0.2 mg.
Biotin 1.4 μg.

Raspberries are high in fibre. Add them to your breakfast cereals in the summer as well as to puddings.

Ratatouille

Portion Two large tablespoons or half a tin.
Weight 200 g., about 7 oz.

Food Facts
Energy 152 kcal.
Protein 1.8 g.
Total fat 12.8 g.
Saturated fat Not known.
Polyunsaturated fat Not known.
Carbohydrate 7.8 g.
Sugars 7.4 g.
Fibre 4.2 g.

Minerals
Calcium 34 mg.
Iron 0.8 mg.
Zinc 0.2 mg.
Copper 0.18 mg.
Sodium 390 mg.
Potassium 536 mg.
Magnesium 28 mg.
Phosphorus 46 mg.

Vitamins
Vitamin A 61 μg.
Vitamin C 10 mg.
Vitamin D None.
Vitamin E 0.8 mg.
Vitamin B1 0.08 mg.
Vitamin B2 0.06 mg.
Niacin 1.8 mg.
Vitamin B6 0.22 mg.
Vitamin B12 None.
Folic acid 44 μg.
Pantothenic acid 0.4 mg.
Biotin None.

When properly made without too much fat, this is a tasty and relatively low calorie vegetable dish.

Rhubarb

Portion One serving stewed without sugar. Raw weight ½ lb. before trimming.

Weight 150 g., about 4¼ oz.

Food Facts
Energy 9 kcal.
Protein 0.9 g.
Total fat None.
Saturated fat None.
Polyunsaturated fat None.
Carbohydrate 1.35 g.
Sugars 1.35 g.
Fibre 3.6 g.

Minerals
Calcium 139 mg.
Iron 0.6 mg.
Zinc 0.16 mg.
Copper 0.18 mg.
Sodium 3 mg.
Potassium 600 mg.
Magnesium 19.5 mg.
Phosphorus 28 mg.

Vitamins
Vitamin A 13.7 μg.
Vitamin C 12 mg.
Vitamin D None.
Vitamin E 0.3 mg.
Vitamin B1 None.
Vitamin B2 0.04 mg.
Niacin 0.45 mg.
Vitamin B6 0.03 mg.
Vitamin B12 None.
Folic acid 6 μg.
Pantothenic acid 0.09 mg.
Biotin Not known.

Rhubarb makes an excellent low calorie high-fibre dessert. Don't just use it in crumbles and pies, eat on its own or with plain yoghurt.

Runner beans

Portion Two tablespoons, cooked.

Weight 100 g., about 3½ oz.

Food Facts
Energy 19 kcal.
Protein 1.9 g.
Total fat 0.2 g.
Saturated fat Not known.
Polyunsaturated fat Not known.
Carbohydrate 2.7 g.
Sugars 1.3 g.
Fibre 3.4 g.

Minerals
Calcium 22 mg.
Iron 0.7 mg.
Zinc 0.3 mg.
Copper 0.05 mg.
Sodium 1 mg.
Potassium 150 mg.
Magnesium 17 mg.
Phosphorus 41 mg.

Vitamins
Vitamin A 66.5 μg.
Vitamin C 5 mg.
Vitamin D None.
Vitamin E 0.2 mg.
Vitamin B1 0.03 mg.
Vitamin B2 0.07 mg.
Niacin 0.8 mg.
Vitamin B6 0.04 mg.
Vitamin B12 None.
Folic acid 28 μg.
Pantothenic acid None.
Biotin 0.5 μg.

Runner beans, like many vegetables, are very low in calories.

Spinach

Portion One average serving of a heaped tablespoon.
Weight 100 g., about 3½ oz.

Food Facts
Energy 30 kcal.
Protein 5.1 g.
Total fat 0.5 g.
Saturated fat Not known.
Polyunsaturated fat Not known.
Carbohydrate 1.4 g.
Sugars 1.2 g.
Fibre 6.3 g.

Minerals
Calcium 600 mg.
Iron 4 mg.
Zinc 0.4 mg.
Copper 0.26 mg.
Sodium 120 mg.
Potassium 490 mg.
Magnesium 59 mg.
Phosphorus 93 mg.

Vitamins
Vitamin A 1,000 μg.
Vitamin C 25 mg.
Vitamin D None.
Vitamin E 2 mg.
Vitamin B1 0.07 mg.
Vitamin B2 0.15 mg.
Niacin 1.8 mg.
Vitamin B6 0.18 mg.
Vitamin B12 None.
Folic acid 140 μg.
Pantothenic acid 0.2 mg.
Biotin 0.1 μg.

This vegetable is very rich in vitamins and minerals and can be added to many main course dishes.

Spring greens

Portion Half a large bunch or a small one of about four leaves.
Weight 40 g., about 1½ oz.

Food Facts
Energy 4 kcal.
Protein 0.7 g.
Total fat None.
Saturated fat None.
Polyunsaturated fat None.
Carbohydrate 0.4 g.
Sugars 0.4 g.
Fibre 1.5 g.

Minerals
Calcium 34.4 mg.
Iron 0.5 mg.
Zinc 0.16 mg.
Copper 0.03 mg.
Sodium 4 mg.
Potassium 48 mg.
Magnesium 3.6 mg.
Phosphorus 12.4 mg.

Vitamins
Vitamin A 266 μg.
Vitamin C 12 mg.
Vitamin D None.
Vitamin E 0.44 mg.
Vitamin B1 0.02 mg.
Vitamin B2 0.08 mg.
Niacin 0.32 mg.
Vitamin B6 0.06 mg.
Vitamin B12 None.
Folic acid 44 μg.
Pantothenic acid 0.1 mg.
Biotin 0.2 μg.

Do not add any sodium bicarbonate to the cooking water. Greens will keep their colour by quick cooking in a small amount of water.

Strawberries

Portion Ten strawberries.

Weight 120 g., about 4 oz.

Food Facts
Energy 31 kcal.
Protein 0.7 g.
Total fat None.
Saturated fat None.
Polyunsaturated fat None.
Carbohydrate 7.4 g.
Sugars 7.4 g.
Fibre 2.6 g.

Minerals
Calcium 26.4 mg.
Iron 0.84 mg.
Zinc 0.12 mg.
Copper 0.16 mg.
Sodium 2.4 mg.
Potassium 192 mg.
Magnesium 14.4 mg.
Phosphorus 27.6 mg.

Vitamins
Vitamin A 6 μg.
Vitamin C 72 mg.
Vitamin D None.
Vitamin E 0.24 mg.
Vitamin B1 0.02 mg.
Vitamin B2 0.04 mg.
Niacin 0.6 mg.
Vitamin B6 0.07 mg.
Vitamin B12 None.
Folic acid 24 μg.
Pantothenic acid 0.4 mg.
Biotin 1.3 μg.

Strawberries are low in calories as well as containing a lot of vitamin C. They taste just as good without sugar or cream.

Sultanas

Portion One handful of about thirty sultanas.

Weight 15 g., about ½ oz.

Food Facts
Energy 37 kcal.
Protein 0.3 g.
Total fat None.
Saturated fat None.
Polyunsaturated fat None.
Carbohydrate 9.7 g.
Sugars 9.7 g.
Fibre 1.05 g.

Minerals
Calcium 7.8 mg.
Iron 0.27 mg.
Zinc 0.01 mg.
Copper 0.05 mg.
Sodium 7.9 mg.
Potassium 129 mg.
Magnesium 5.2 mg.
Phosphorus 14.2 mg.

Vitamins
Vitamin A 0.7 μg.
Vitamin C None.
Vitamin D None.
Vitamin E 0.1 mg.
Vitamin B1 0.01 mg.
Vitamin B2 0.01 mg.
Niacin 0.09 mg.
Vitamin B6 0.04 mg.
Vitamin B12 None.
Folic acid 0.6 μg.
Pantothenic acid None.
Biotin Not known.

Adding a few sultanas to stewed fruit will make it more interesting. Give them to children instead of sweets.

Swede

Portion 1½ tablespoons mashed. About ⅛ medium sized swede.

Weight 100 g., about 3½ oz.

Food Facts
Energy 18 kcal.
Protein 0.9 g.
Total fat None.
Saturated fat None.
Polyunsaturated fat None.
Carbohydrate 3.8 g.
Sugars 3.7 g.
Fibre 2.8 g.

Minerals
Calcium 42 mg.
Iron 0.3 mg.
Zinc Not known.
Copper 0.04 mg.
Sodium 14 mg.
Potassium 100 mg.
Magnesium 7 mg.
Phosphorus 18 mg.

Vitamins
Vitamin A None.
Vitamin C 17 mg.
Vitamin D None.
Vitamin E None.
Vitamin B1 0.04 mg.
Vitamin B2 0.03 mg.
Niacin 0.8 mg.
Vitamin B6 0.12 mg.
Vitamin B12 None.
Folic acid 21 μg.
Pantothenic acid 0.07 mg.
Biotin None.

If you normally mash swede, do not add butter but you can use plenty of black pepper.

Sweet potato

Portion The size of two large eggs.

Weight 130 g., about 4½ oz.

Food Facts
Energy 110 kcal.
Protein 1.4 g.
Total fat 0.8 g.
Saturated fat Not known.
Polyunsaturated fat Not known.
Carbohydrate 26 g.
Sugars 11.8 g.
Fibre 3 g.

Minerals
Calcium 27.3 mg.
Iron 0.78 mg.
Zinc Not known.
Copper 0.19 mg.
Sodium 23.4 mg.
Potassium 390 mg.
Magnesium 15.6 mg.
Phosphorus 57.2 mg.

Vitamins
Vitamin A 866 μg.
Vitamin C 19.5 mg.
Vitamin D None.
Vitamin E 5.2 mg.
Vitamin B1 0.1 mg.
Vitamin B2 0.05 mg.
Niacin 1.17 mg.
Vitamin B6 0.17 mg.
Vitamin B12 None.
Folic acid 32.5 μg.
Pantothenic acid 0.9 mg.
Biotin Not known.

Use instead of ordinary potatoes baked in their jackets. An acquired taste becoming more popular in the UK.

Sweetcorn

Portion One heaped tablespoon, tinned.
Weight 100 g., about 3½ oz.

Food Facts
Energy 76 kcal.
Protein 2.9 g.
Total fat 0.5 g.
Saturated fat Not known.
Polyunsaturated fat Not known.
Carbohydrate 16.1 g.
Sugars 8.9 g.
Fibre 5.7 g.

Minerals
Calcium 3 mg.
Iron 0.6 mg.
Zinc 0.6 mg.
Copper 0.05 mg.
Sodium 310 mg.
Potassium 200 mg.
Magnesium 23 mg.
Phosphorus 67 mg.

Vitamins
Vitamin A 210 μg.
Vitamin C 5 mg.
Vitamin D None.
Vitamin E 0.5 mg.
Vitamin B1 0.05 mg.
Vitamin B2 0.08 mg.
Niacin 1.5 mg.
Vitamin B6 0.16 mg.
Vitamin B12 None.
Folic acid 32 μg.
Pantothenic acid 0.2 mg.
Biotin Not known.

Use small amounts of sweetcorn to add colour to salads. Avoid eating a lot of it if you are trying to lose weight.

Tangerine

Portion One medium-sized, peeled.
Weight 70 g., about 2½ oz.

Food Facts
Energy 23 kcal.
Protein 0.6 g.
Total fat None.
Saturated fat None.
Polyunsaturated fat None.
Carbohydrate 5.6 g.
Sugars 5.6 g.
Fibre 1.3 g.

Minerals
Calcium 29.4 mg.
Iron 0.21 mg.
Zinc 0.07 mg.
Copper 0.06 mg.
Sodium 1.4 mg.
Potassium 112 mg.
Magnesium 7.7 mg.
Phosphorus 11.9 mg.

Vitamins
Vitamin A 11.5 μg.
Vitamin C 21 mg.
Vitamin D None.
Vitamin E Not known.
Vitamin B1 0.05 mg.
Vitamin B2 0.01 mg.
Niacin 0.21 mg.
Vitamin B6 0.05 mg.
Vitamin B12 None.
Folic acid 14.7 μg.
Pantothenic acid 0.1 mg.
Biotin Not known.

Tangerines make a welcome change from oranges but contain less vitamin C.

Tinned fruit salad

Portion One bowlful.

Weight 130 g., about 4½ oz.

Food Facts
Energy 123 kcal.
Protein 0.4 g.
Total fat None.
Saturated fat None.
Polyunsaturated fat None.
Carbohydrate 32.5 g.
Sugars 32.5 g.
Fibre 1.4 g.

Minerals
Calcium 10.4 mg.
Iron 1.3 mg.
Zinc Not known.
Copper 0.04 mg.
Sodium 2.6 mg.
Potassium 156 mg.
Magnesium 10.4 mg.
Phosphorus 13 mg.

Vitamins
Vitamin A 65 μg.
Vitamin C 3.9 mg.
Vitamin D None.
Vitamin E Not known.
Vitamin B1 0.03 mg.
Vitamin B2 0.01 mg.
Niacin 0.39 mg.
Vitamin B6 0.01 mg.
Vitamin B12 None.
Folic acid 5.2 μg.
Pantothenic acid 0.1 mg.
Biotin 0.1 μg.

Tinned fruit salad contains twice the calories and half the fibre of fresh fruit salad. Buy tins without added sugar.

Tofu, soya bean curd

Portion One steamed cube 2 in. × 2 in. × 1 in.

Weight 140 g., about 5 oz.

Food Facts
Energy 98 kcal.
Protein 10.3 g.
Total fat 5.8 g.
Saturated fat Not known.
Polyunsaturated fat Not known.
Carbohydrate 0.84 g.
Sugars Not known.
Fibre 0.42 g.

Minerals
Calcium 709 mg.
Iron 1.6 mg.
Zinc 0.98 mg.
Copper 2.3 mg.
Sodium 5.6 mg.
Potassium 88 mg.
Magnesium 32 mg.
Phosphorus Not known.

Vitamins
Vitamin A None.
Vitamin C None.
Vitamin D None.
Vitamin E Not known.
Vitamin B1 0.08 mg.
Vitamin B2 0.02 mg.
Niacin 0.14 mg.
Vitamin B6 Not known.
Vitamin B12 None.
Folic acid Not known.
Pantothenic acid Not known.
Biotin Not known.

Add tofu to vegetable casseroles or stir-fried dishes to increase the protein content.

Tomato, raw

Portion One medium-sized tomato.
Weight 75 g., about 2¾oz.

Food Facts

Energy 10 kcal.
Protein 0.7 g.
Total fat None.
Saturated fat None.
Polyunsaturated fat None.
Carbohydrate 2.1 g.
Sugars 2.1 g.
Fibre 1.1 g.

Minerals

Calcium 9.7 mg.
Iron 0.3 mg.
Zinc 0.15 mg.
Copper 0.07 mg.
Sodium 2.2 mg.
Potassium 217 mg.
Magnesium 8.2 mg.
Phosphorus 15.7 mg.

Vitamins

Vitamin A 75 µg.
Vitamin C 15 mg.
Vitamin D None.
Vitamin E 0.9 mg.
Vitamin B1 0.04 mg.
Vitamin B2 0.03 mg.
Niacin 0.6 mg.
Vitamin B6 0.08 mg.
Vitamin B12 None.
Folic acid 21 µg.
Pantothenic acid 0.2 mg.
Biotin 1.1 µg.

Fresh tomatoes make a tasty snack or sandwich filling all year round.

Tomato, fried

Portion One medium-sized tomato fried in butter.
Weight 69 g., about 2½ oz.

Food Facts

Energy 46 kcal.
Protein 0.69 g.
Total fat 4 g.
Saturated fat 1.9 g.
Polyunsaturated fat 0.08 g.
Carbohydrate 2.2 g.
Sugars 2.2 g.
Fibre Not known.

Minerals

Calcium 10.3 mg.
Iron 0.34 mg.
Zinc 0.13 mg.
Copper 0.07 mg.
Sodium 2.0 mg.
Potassium 233 mg.
Magnesium 8.8 mg.
Phosphorus 17.2 mg.

Vitamins

Vitamin A None.
Vitamin C 6.9 mg.
Vitamin D None.
Vitamin E Not known.
Vitamin B1 Not known.
Vitamin B2 Not known.
Niacin 0.06 mg.
Vitamin B6 Not known.
Vitamin B12 None.
Folic acid Not known.
Pantothenic acid Not known.
Biotin Not known.

Try grilling or baking tomatoes instead of frying to reduce your fat intake.

Tomatoes, tinned

Portion Half a medium-sized tin.

Weight 200 g., about 7 oz.

Food Facts
Energy 24 kcal.
Protein 2.2 g.
Total fat None.
Saturated fat None.
Polyunsaturated fat None.
Carbohydrate 4 g.
Sugars 4 g.
Fibre 1.8 g.

Minerals
Calcium 18 mg.
Iron 1.8 mg.
Zinc 0.6 mg.
Copper 0.22 mg.
Sodium 58 mg.
Potassium 540 mg.
Magnesium 22 mg.
Phosphorus 44 mg.

Vitamins
Vitamin A 167 μg.
Vitamin C 36 mg.
Vitamin D None.
Vitamin E 2.4 mg.
Vitamin B1 0.12 mg.
Vitamin B2 0.06 mg.
Niacin 1.6 mg.
Vitamin B6 0.22 mg.
Vitamin B12 None.
Folic acid 50 μg.
Pantothenic acid 0.4 mg.
Biotin 3 μg.

Tinned tomatoes make an excellent base for many dishes. A tomato sauce is a good substitute for a milk-based sauce.

Tomato puree

Portion One tablespoon.

Weight 15 g., about ½ oz.

Food Facts
Energy 10 kcal.
Protein 0.9 g.
Total fat None.
Saturated fat None.
Polyunsaturated fat None.
Carbohydrate 1.7 g.
Sugars 1.7 g.
Fibre Not known.

Minerals
Calcium 7.6 mg.
Iron 0.76 mg.
Zinc 0.25 mg.
Copper 0.09 mg.
Sodium 3 mg.
Potassium 231 mg.
Magnesium 9.9 mg.
Phosphorus 19.5 mg.

Vitamins
Vitamin A 71.5 μg.
Vitamin C 15 mg.
Vitamin D None.
Vitamin E 1.03 mg.
Vitamin B1 0.05 mg.
Vitamin B2 0.03 mg.
Niacin 0.72 mg.
Vitamin B6 0.09 mg.
Vitamin B12 None.
Folic acid 21 μg.
Pantothenic acid 0.2 mg.
Biotin 1.2 μg.

Add tomato puree to soups and stews. It will thicken them without increasing the calorie value.

Turnip

Portion One turnip the size of a tennis ball, boiled.
Weight 100 g., about 3½ oz.

Food Facts

Energy 14 kcal.
Protein 0.7 g.
Total fat 0.3 g.
Saturated fat Not known.
Polyunsaturated fat Not known.
Carbohydrate 2.3 g.
Sugars 2.3 g.
Fibre 2.2 g.

Minerals

Calcium 55 mg.
Iron 0.4 mg.
Zinc Not known.
Copper 0.04 mg.
Sodium 28 mg.
Potassium 160 mg.
Magnesium 7 mg.
Phosphorus 19 mg.

Vitamins

Vitamin A None.
Vitamin C 17 mg.
Vitamin D None.
Vitamin E None.
Vitamin B1 0.03 mg.
Vitamin B2 0.04 mg.
Niacin 0.6 mg.
Vitamin B6 0.06 mg.
Vitamin B12 None.
Folic acid 10 μg.
Pantothenic acid 0.1 mg.
Biotin None.

Try turnips as a change from parsnips. They only take a few minutes to cook and contain fewer calories.

Vegetable curry

Portion One serving, about two to three tablespoons.
Weight 200 g., about 7 oz.

Food Facts

Energy 362 kcal.
Protein 3.6 g.
Total fat 30.4 g.
Saturated fat Not known.
Polyunsaturated fat Not known.
Carbohydrate 20 g.
Sugars Not known.
Fibre Not known.

Minerals

Calcium 78 mg.
Iron 1.6 mg.
Zinc 0.6 mg.
Copper 0.24 mg.
Sodium 896 mg.
Potassium 832 mg.
Magnesium 42 mg.
Phosphorus Not known.

Vitamins

Vitamin A 1,426 μg.
Vitamin C 24 mg.
Vitamin D 0.2 μg.
Vitamin E Not known.
Vitamin B1 0.14 mg.
Vitamin B2 0.1 mg.
Niacin 2.2 mg.
Vitamin B6 Not known.
Vitamin B12 None.
Folic acid 30 μg.
Pantothenic acid Not known.
Biotin Not known.

Vegetable curry is best made at home using as little oil as possible. Curry spices have no calorie value.

Walnuts

Portion Six walnut halves.

Weight 20 g., about ⅔ oz.

Food Facts
Energy 105 kcal.
Protein 2.1 g.
Total fat 10.3 g.
Saturated fat 1.1 g.
Polyunsaturated fat 7.3 g.
Carbohydrate 1 g.
Sugars 0.6 g.
Fibre 1 g.

Minerals
Calcium 12 mg.
Iron 0.48 mg.
Zinc 0.6 mg.
Copper 0.06 mg.
Sodium 0.6 mg.
Potassium 138 mg.
Magnesium 26 mg.
Phosphorus 102 mg.

Vitamins
Vitamin A None.
Vitamin C None.
Vitamin D None.
Vitamin E 0.16 mg.
Vitamin B1 0.06 mg.
Vitamin B2 0.02 mg.
Niacin 0.2 mg.
Vitamin B6 0.15 mg.
Vitamin B12 None.
Folic acid 13.2 μg.
Pantothenic acid 0.18 mg.
Biotin 0.4 μg.

70% of the fat contained in walnuts is polyunsaturated fat. In other nuts the amount is usually 30% or less.

Watercress

Portion One quarter of an average bunch.

Weight 20 g., about ⅔ oz.

Food Facts
Energy 2 kcal.
Protein 0.6 g.
Total fat None.
Saturated fat None.
Polyunsaturated fat None.
Carbohydrate 0.1 g.
Sugars 0.1 g.
Fibre 0.7 g.

Minerals
Calcium 44 mg.
Iron 0.32 mg.
Zinc 0.04 mg.
Copper 0.03 mg.
Sodium 12 mg.
Potassium 62 mg.
Magnesium 3.4 mg.
Phosphorus 10.4 mg.

Vitamins
Vitamin A 100 μg.
Vitamin C 12 mg.
Vitamin D None.
Vitamin E 0.2 mg.
Vitamin B1 0.02 mg.
Vitamin B2 0.02 mg.
Niacin 0.22 mg.
Vitamin B6 0.03 mg.
Vitamin B12 None.
Folic acid Not known.
Pantothenic acid None.
Biotin 0.1 μg.

Watercress adds a lot of flavour and colour to soups and salads. It also makes a good sandwich filling.

Watermelon

Portion One slice without pips or skin.
Weight 180 g., about 6½ oz.

Food Facts
Energy 37 kcal.
Protein 0.7 g.
Total fat None.
Saturated fat None.
Polyunsaturated fat None.
Carbohydrate 9.5 g.
Sugars 9.5 g.
Fibre 1.6 g.

Minerals
Calcium 9 mg.
Iron 0.54 mg.
Zinc 0.18 mg.
Copper 0.05 mg.
Sodium 7.2 mg.
Potassium 216 mg.
Magnesium 19.8 mg.
Phosphorus 14.4 mg.

Vitamins
Vitamin A 6.3 μg.
Vitamin C 9 mg.
Vitamin D None.
Vitamin E 0.18 mg.
Vitamin B1 0.04 mg.
Vitamin B2 0.04 mg.
Niacin 0.54 mg.
Vitamin B6 0.13 mg.
Vitamin B12 None.
Folic acid 5.4 μg.
Pantothenic acid 2.8 mg.
Biotin Not known.

Watermelon tastes very sweet but one large slice contains less calories than most other fruits. Try it instead of other melons for a change.

Yam

Portion The size of a medium potato, boiled.
Weight 130 g., about 4½ oz.

Food Facts
Energy 154 kcal.
Protein 2.1 g.
Total fat 0.1 g.
Saturated fat Not known.
Polyunsaturated fat Not known.
Carbohydrate 38 g.
Sugars 0.3 g.
Fibre 5.1 g.

Minerals
Calcium 11.7 mg.
Iron 0.39 mg.
Zinc 0.52 mg.
Copper 0.19 mg.
Sodium 22.1 mg.
Potassium 390 mg.
Magnesium 18.2 mg.
Phosphorus 42.9 mg.

Vitamins
Vitamin A 2.6 μg.
Vitamin C 2.6 mg.
Vitamin D None.
Vitamin E Not known.
Vitamin B1 0.06 mg.
Vitamin B2 0.01 mg.
Niacin 1.04 mg.
Vitamin B6 Not known.
Vitamin B12 None.
Folic acid 7.8 μg.
Pantothenic acid 0.6 mg.
Biotin Not known.

Yams should be eaten and cooked like potatoes but contain more calories.

Index